Storming The Gates Of Hell

--Action in Acts

Storming The Gates Of Hell

--Action in Acts

Howard F. Sugden

ACCENT BOOKS
Denver, Colorado

MEMBER OF
EVANGELICAL CHRISTIAN
PUBLISHERS ASSOCIATION

ACCENT BOOKS
A division of B/P Publications
12100 W. Sixth Avenue
P.O. Box 15337
Denver, Colorado 80215

Library of Congress Catalog Card Number: 75-50296

ISBN O-916406-63-6

CONTENTS

1. Ingredients for Action **7**

2. Power for Action **18**

3. Program for Action **28**

4. Assault through Authority **38**

5. Action through Organization **49**

6. Vision for Action **59**

7. Getting Past the Wall **70**

8. Dynamic Changes **80**

9. Divine Intervention **90**

10. Storming through God's Direction **99**

11. Action through Guidance **108**

12. Action through Affirmation **118**

CHAPTER 1
Ingredients for Action

*W*hen I was a boy on the farm, Saturday was a great day. Two unusual events took place on that day. At the determined hour on Saturday all four of us boys lined up for the bath. For many years, whenever I heard the term, "Knights of the Bath," I thought it was a clear reference to Saturday nights. More important to my thinking than the bath was what happened earlier in the day on Saturday. From our big kitchen came the rattle of pans that said, "This is bake day." When we stepped into the kitchen we found mother with her mixing bowl (without benefit of cake mix—or any other mix). Arranged before her were all the ingredients that would find their way into the bowl, into the oven and into our appreciative stomachs. Mother's cooking would satisfy the most ardent connoisseur's taste.

In the first chapter of the book of Acts, we are confronted with the living Christ, and we see Him arranging the ingredients to be used by the church when she stepped out of the womb of Heaven into history.

Have you ever thought of the ancient world around that early church? It was a world of slavery, with two slaves to every free man.

Added to the problem of bondage was the problem of a welfare state, with hundreds of thousands of Roman citizens receiving free grain. It was a period of leisure, when over one hundred days each year were given over to sports at staggering cost to the government. It was a time when Romans indulged their excessive physical and social appetites. Gluttony and laziness among the Romans were unmatched anywhere else in the world. Of course the Romans achieved some remarkable feats in spite of their faults. For example, they tied their empire together with a network of 47,000 miles of good roads.

This strikes me as a true analogy of today's world. And it was into this desperate culture that God, with sovereign hand, flung a new society to move against the tide and turn the course of human history. As I read and re-read the book of Acts there is a growing desire in my heart that the church—your church, my church—might find the secret these early believers used to turn the world right side up. We need the empowerment that was theirs, so that in an equally desperate day we might do the impossible.

The Ingredient of Knowledge

In a confused world, the early Christians moved with certainty because they had met Jesus Christ. Dr. Luke, the author of Acts, is careful to emphasize this. "To whom also he shewed himself alive after his passion by many infallible proofs, being seen of them forty days, and speaking of the things pertaining to the kingdom of God" (Acts 1:3). They had stood together on that hill outside Jerusalem, had seen the uplifted cross, had felt hope die within them. They had gone to Joseph's tomb and found it empty, and knew that their Master was beyond the reach of death—that He lived by the power of an endless life.

The difference between defeat and victory rests in knowing Jesus Christ in this way. Life begins at this point. "He that hath the Son hath life; and he that hath not the Son of God hath not life" (I John 5:12).

F. Paxton Hood's hymn, "Jesus Lives and Jesus Leads," links this fact of resurrection with our needs in these words:

Jesus lives, and Jesus leads,
Tho' the way be dreary;
Morn to darkest nights succeeds,
Courage, then, ye weary:
Still the faithful shepherd feeds;
Jesus lives and Jesus leads.

With this priceless ingredient of knowing the risen Christ every believer is fitted to serve the living God.

The Ingredient of Fellowship

The Spirit of God brings before us in Acts 1:4 a truth which is so important to the life of the church, "And, being assembled together with them...." This might also be understood to mean "eating with them" where we read "assembled together." The Lord of life and glory shared the common experiences of human life. We miss everything if we miss this.

Recently I drove hundreds of miles through England and Scotland, visiting the great cathedrals. My heart was filled with awe at their majesty and grandeur. But we miss the wonder of the Lord's greatness if we do not see Him involved in the ordinary experiences of our lives. He came to Mary in the garden. He walked along the seashores. He trod the road to Emmaus to meet with lonely disciples.

When Eric Marshall and Stuart Hample set out to discover what children thought of God, the results were intriguing. You may read their findings in the lovely little volume, *God Is a Good Friend to Have.* One thoughtful youngster spoke what many misguided persons seem to believe. The child volunteered, "God is always around when you need help. But only with important things. Not your homework."

We should whisper in the child's ear: "You're wrong, child. He's interested in your homework too!"

The forty days of Christ's walk with His disciples draws to a close. He has proven Himself alive. He has entered in and shared in the common experiences of life.

The Ingredient of Anticipation

When John, under divine direction, gave us the fourth Gospel, he recorded a delightful evening scene in chapter 13. The shadows of the cross were beginning to fall across the path of our Lord. In a few days He would "make his soul an offering for sin" (Isaiah 53:10), then return to the Father. John's word is a fragrant one. "Jesus knowing that the Father had given all things into his hands, and that he was come from God, and went to God . . ." (John 13:3). It is evident that our Lord moved along the roads of Palestine with an anticipation in His heart of that day when He would return to His Father's house. That day had arrived when Jesus and His disciples stood on the hill outside Jerusalem.

There is a quiet majesty about our Lord's ascension. "He was parted from them and carried up into heaven" (Luke 24:51). Mark says, "He was received up into heaven" (Mark 16:19). This scene in Acts 1:9-11 is unforgettable—the ascending Lord, the embracing cloud, the angelic attendants, and the words from Heaven, "Ye men of Galilee, why stand ye gazing up into heaven? this same Jesus, which is taken up from you into heaven, shall so come in like manner as ye have seen him go into heaven." And while angelic hosts cry, "Lift up your heads, O ye gates; and be ye lift up, ye everlasting doors; and the King of glory shall come in" (Psalm 24:7), there is the triumphant announcement to those below, "He will be back!"

When this truth takes hold of us we can never be the same again. There may be dark and restless nights, the sky above may be black and threatening, the burdens of life may mount up, the pressures may become almost unbearable. But the promise is there: He will return. It gives us courage and hope as we anticipate its fulfillment.

The great Joseph Parker, reflecting upon this promise suggested: "Looking up is God's medicine for wounded hearts and bruised lives. A young soldier on the battlefield of World War II fell amidst bursting shells and drone of planes. It was Good Friday. In his wounded condition he tried unsuccessfully to signal passing planes. He slipped away into unconsciousness, and when he awakened he was in the field hospital with a chaplain leaning over him.

'How did you endure?' asked the chaplain.

'You can endure anything on Good Friday,' came the quick response, 'because you know there's an Easter.'"

Anticipation of our risen Lord's return is God's answer for us in a weary and decadent age as surely as it was His answer for the first-century disciples.

As the ascension scene of Acts 1:9 ends, the trailing clouds of glory are lost against the deep blue sky. *He will be back* will cheer His friends—the disciples—in dark and lonely hours. So the disciples return to Jerusalem to tarry for the "promise of the Father."

The Ingredient of Obedience

Have you ever surveyed the book of Acts with the thought of discovering the secret of men who move triumphantly against the forces of a pagan society? When the risen Christ told His disciples to wait for the promise of the Father they could have appointed a committee to try to discover some hidden meaning in His words. They could have asked: "Shall we take what He said figuratively, spiritually or literally?" But they didn't. They took the promise at face value and acted upon it. With the wonder of the living Christ before them they returned to Jerusalem to obey His command.

If there is one key that unlocks the treasures of Heaven for us, it is the key marked "obedience." The opening chapters of Acts show how obedient Christ's followers were. When the authorities pushed the apostles into the common prison, God dispatched an angel who told them to "Go . . . stand . . . speak." They did just that. Apprehended again and threatened, Peter and the other apostles cried out, "We ought to obey

God rather than men" (Acts 5:29). They delivered the gospel message in obedience to God. It could well be that the world today is seldom startled at our presence because we have lost the wonder of obedience in our ministry.

When Philip the evangelist was experiencing showers of blessing upon the ministry of the Word in Samaria, he received a communication from Heaven to depart from the place of blessing and go to the desert. It must have been difficult for him to leave without a farewell (to say nothing of the love offering). However, his obedience brought him in touch with an Ethiopian prince whose opened heart resulted in Ethiopia stretching out her hands to God.

Eusebius (A. D. 265-340), in his *Ecclesiastical History*, throws light upon the result of Philip's obedience to God's will with these words: "For as the annunciation of the Saviour's Gospel was daily advancing, by a certain divine providence, a prince of the queen of the Ethiopians, as it is a custom that still prevails there to be governed by a female, was brought thither, and was the first of the Gentiles that received of the mysteries of the divine word from Philip. The Apostle, led by a vision, thus instructed him and he, becoming the first fruits of believers throughout the world, is said to have been the first on returning to his own country, that proclaimed the knowledge of God and the salutary abode of our Saviour among men. If that is fact, the prophecy obtained its ful-

filment through him, 'Ethiopia stretcheth
forth her hands unto God'" (Psalm 68:31).

As we observe obedience in the life of the
early church, we must not miss the dramatic
scene in which the Apostle Paul stood before
wicked Agrippa to state, "I was not dis-
obedient unto the heavenly vision" (Acts
26:19).

The Ingredient of Communication

In the midst of the swift-moving events in
Acts chapter 1, we hear the voices of believers
in prayer. I am glad their prayers weren't
recorded, for if they had been we would be
repeating them like a dog's bark. Obviously,
the lines of communication between the
believers and God were unclogged, fresh,
clear. And isn't this how our own prayer life
should be? Perhaps Peter was reflecting upon
those early days when he wrote in his first
letter that God's ears are open to the prayers
of His people (I Peter 3:12).

The prayer life of the early church demonstrated clearly that the divine life within the
believers was calling out to the One who had
bestowed eternal life upon them. Their
prayers showed how much they counted upon
God. When they were threatened by the
authorities, they prayed and the meeting
place was shaken (Acts 4:23-31). When one of
their number was marked for death, the hand
of prayer touched Heaven and prison doors
were unlocked by the hand that flung out

worlds (Acts 12:7-15). When it appeared that the ministry which had opened in Europe would be hindered by the arrest of those who had come with the message, God's *Amen* to the prayer of Paul and Silas shook not only the prison but also the hard heart of their jailor (Acts 16:25-29).

The Ingredient of Understanding

Tragedy had walked into the apostolic company, gathered together in Acts 1. One of their number had defected. It was common talk in the streets. "Did you hear about Judas?" It was essential that his place be filled, and there were two qualified men to choose between. The future ministry of the apostles would, in great measure, rest upon their decision. Sensing the seriousness of the situation, the believers cried, "Thou Lord, which knowest . . . show" (Acts 1:24).

In the midst of life's conflicts, pressures, and frustrations, there is One who knows. When Job felt roughed up by the heavy hands of adversity he spoke with confidence, "But he knoweth the way that I take" (Job 23:10). David, who may have heard of the death of a friend, spoke this encouraging word, "The Lord knoweth the days of the upright" (Psalm 37:18). How often comfort has poured into my heart as I meditated upon the words of the sweet singer: "For he knoweth our frame; he remembereth that we are dust" (Psalm 103:14).

The early believers made their decisions

with calm hearts because they found that the Lord knew, understood, and was able to do "exceeding abundantly above all that we ask or think" (Ephesians 3:20).

> *I know not what awaits me:*
> *God kindly veils mine eyes,*
> *And o'er each step of my onward way*
> *He makes new scenes to rise;*
> *And every joy He sends me comes*
> *A sweet and glad surprise.*
> *Where He may lead I'll follow,*
> *My trust in Him repose;*
> *And every hour in perfect peace*
> *I'll sing, He knows! He knows!*
> —Mary G. Brainerd

CHAPTER 2
Power for Action

*C*hrist's coming into the world was absolutely unparalleled.

He alone spoke before He was born. "Wherefore when he cometh into the world, he saith, Sacrifice and offering thou wouldest not, but a body hast thou prepared me: In burnt-offerings and sacrifices for sin thou hast had no pleasure. Then said I, Lo, I come (in the volume of the book it is written of me,) to do thy will, O God" (Hebrews 10:5-7). In the will of God, that prepared body was born in a manger, walked the dusty roads of Palestine, rode over stormy seas, and "was in all points tempted like as we are, yet without sin" (Hebrews 4:15).

In that body Jesus was led away under an Eastern sky to make His soul an offering for sin (Isaiah 53:10). *He was the only man in history who could affirm that He had finished the work God gave Him to do* (John 17:4). His work on the cross would result in a redeemed people—from both Jews and Gentiles. He assured those who would be witnesses, "ye shall be baptized with the Holy Ghost not many days hence" (Acts 1:5). As Christ looked across the centuries, He saw every care, every defeat, every frustration, every sorrow, every trial that His people would experience, and against this challenging background He displayed the promise of His infinite power. The risen Christ, possessing all power in Heaven and earth, assured these frail men that one day in the program of God there would be an unleashing of Heaven's power for the redeemed.

Do you remember those early days when your mother was trying to teach you to tell time? You could hardly believe that the Mickey Mouse or the Timex could reveal such wonderful mysteries. When you had mastered the face of the clock, your attention was turned to the calendar on the kitchen wall. Some of the numbers were red, and you learned about extra-special days.

God's Calendar

The eternal, sovereign God has a calendar, and on that calendar He has marked some special days. Let's think for a minute about

God's great days. There was the day when He formed man out of the dust of the ground and breathed into his nostrils the breath of life. What a day that was! Then came the day—after sin entered the world—that God provided a covering for Adam and Eve. And we can't omit the day when God's hand of judgment opened the windows of Heaven and the floods came. You are probably thinking right now of many other days of tremendous consequence on God's calendar, culminating when a Baby was born who was destined to "save his people from their sins" (Matthew 1:21).

There is an atmosphere of excitement as you open the Bible to the book of Acts, a record of "all that Jesus began both to do and teach." And the wonder of it is that what He began will go on and on throughout history through empowered men—empowered when just the right day on God's calendar had arrived.

Today there is a unique vehicle in history that is both *doing* and *teaching*. For over 1900 years she has moved through "toil and tribulation, and tumult of her wars." When did God begin this work that has proceeded triumphantly across the centuries? If we gather together the Scriptures that relate to God's vehicle, the church, we come to the conclusion that in the eyes of God the Church began on the day of Pentecost.

In his book, *Act of the Apostles,* W. Graham Scroggie observes, "There were Christians before Pentecost, but on this day they were constituted the Christian Church by the descent and baptism of the Holy Spirit."

Philip Schaff, in the first volume of his monumental *History of the Christian Church,* states, "The ascension of Christ to heaven was followed ten days afterwards by the descent of the Holy Spirit upon earth and the birth of the Christian Church."

In the eyes of God, who is sovereign in all His ways, a new work was begun in the world at Pentecost, but the Scriptures make it abundantly clear that it was not fully revealed to men at that time. Paul carefully announces, "Unto me, who am less than the least of all saints, is this grace given, that I should preach among the Gentiles the unsearchable riches of Christ, and to make all men see what is the fellowship of the mystery, which from the beginning of the world hath been hid in God, who created all things by Jesus Christ: To the intent that now unto the principalities and powers in heavenly places might be known by the church the manifold wisdom of God" (Ephesians 3:8-11).

A Day of Realized Promise

Isaiah heard a man crying in the wilderness, "Prepare ye the way of the Lord, make straight in the desert a highway for our God. Every valley shall be exalted, and every mountain and hill shall be made low: and the crooked shall be made straight, and the rough places plain: And the glory of the Lord shall be revealed, and all flesh shall see it together:

for the mouth of the Lord hath spoken it" (Isaiah 40:3-5).

Then the time came! There was an air of great expectation as John stood by Jordan to cry, "I indeed baptize you with water unto repentance: but he that cometh after me is mightier than I. . .he shall baptize you with the Holy Ghost and with fire" (Matthew 3:11). The importance of this fact is underscored by all four Gospel writers. (See Mark 1:8; Luke 3:16; John 1:33.)

Following His resurrection the Lord reminded His disciples of a day coming, that John the Baptist had predicted, and He added, ". . .not many days hence" (Acts 1:5). Peter, in Acts 11, was called upon to give an explanation for his going to the Gentiles with the gospel. He explained: "as I began to speak, the Holy Ghost fell on them, as on us at the beginning. Then remembered I the word of the Lord, how that he said, John indeed baptized with water; but ye shall be baptized with the Holy Ghost" (Acts 11:16). Peter had lived to see John the Baptist's prediction fulfilled.

The "beginning" Peter referred to was Pentecost—the day John the Baptist had predicted.

We turn from this aspect of a unique event in history to find that it was also—

A Day of Fulfillment

Luke is careful to tell us that "The day of Pentecost was fully come" (Acts 2:1). What took place on that day fulfilled the picture of the Old Testament Pentecostal feast. It bore the name, "feast of weeks" (Exodus 34:22), "feast of harvest" (Exodus 23:16), "the day of firstfruits" (Numbers 28:26). It was the occasion for offering gratitude to God for the deliverance given from Egyptian bondage (Deuteronomy 16:12).

Thomas Walker's book, *The Acts of the Apostles,* provides valuable help on this. "In every respect. . .the day was a most appropriate one for the descent of the Holy Ghost: a. As the day when a cosmopolitan assembly was gathered at Jerusalem, it provided a grand opportunity for the first great dissemination of the Gospel. b. As the day of the firstfruits, it was a suitable one for the conversion of the three thousand, the firstfruits of a greater harvest yet to be gathered in. c. As the day of commemoration of deliverance from bondage, it illustrated the work of the Holy Ghost, for 'where the Spirit of the Lord is, there is liberty' (2 Corinthians 3:17). d. As the day which, to the later Jews at least, spoke of the promulgation of their great law from Sinai, it was a fitting one for the first great promulgation of the Gospel from Jerusalem by the Holy Ghost sent down from heaven."

We must not forget that this remarkable day of fulfillment took place on the day after the Sabbath (Leviticus 23:15,16). This great truth gives to us, with other Scriptures, the reason for our gathering together on the first day of the week. We are privileged to look in upon a meeting of the early church in Acts

20:6-12. It could well be one of our services in this day. The day was the first day of the week, the purpose was to keep the ordinances and to hear the Word of God. (And Paul reminds the Corinthian believers in I Corinthians 16 not to forget the offering when they gather on this day!)

The wonder of this remarkable day increased as we discover that it was—

A Day of Blessing

There had been many unforgettable occasions in the lives of the apostles during their enrollment in the school of Christ. On one memorable evening He taught them visibly as He moved from disciple to disciple with a towel and a basin, performing the humble, lowly task of washing their feet. He said to them, "What I do thou knowest not now; but thou shalt know hereafter" (John 13:7). He was inviting them to look beyond this occasion to the day when He would ascend to Heaven to keep the feet of all His saints clean.

On that same evening the Lord Jesus repeatedly brought to the disciples' attention the day when He would depart. His departure would signal the beginning of a new work in history. "And I will pray the Father, and he shall give you another Comforter, that he may abide with you forever" (John 14:16). As the disciples struggled to understand His words, He spoke again, "But the Comforter, which is the Holy Ghost, whom the Father will send in my name, he shall teach you all things, and bring all things to your remembrance, whatsoever I have said unto you" (John 14:26).

When Peter on the day of Pentecost heard the sound of a rushing mighty wind and saw the cloven tongues like as of fire, he realized that this event fulfilled Christ's promises about the coming of the Spirit. In his first great sermon Peter proclaimed the fact that Jesus Christ had arrived in Heaven, had prayed to the Father, and the Spirit of God had come (Acts 2:32,33).

On this important day there were two definite moves of the Spirit of God. First, He came to baptize believers into the one body (I Corinthians 12:13). Peter affirmed in Acts 11:16 that Pentecost fulfilled the Gospels' prediction of the baptism of the Holy Spirit. Before Pentecost the followers of Christ were individual believers without corporate union. But the baptism of the Spirit on the day of Pentecost changed that. From Pentecost on they were a united body of believers.

Dr. A. C. Gaebelein, in *The Acts of the Apostles,* has a word worth considering: "All believers were on that day [Pentecost] united into the one body, and since then, whenever and wherever a sinner believes in the finished work of Christ, he shares in that baptism, and is joined by the same Spirit to that one body. A believer may be in dense ignorance about all this, as indeed a great many are, but this does not alter the gracious fact of what God has done. The believing company was then formed on the day of Pentecost into one body. It was the birthday of the Church."

For many years I have offered to those who are interested in the baptizing work of the Spirit of God a substantial reward if they can produce in the Word of God any definite command to be *baptized* by the Spirit. To this present hour no one has come forward with such proof. The reason is that there is no such command. The baptism of the Spirit is non-experiential. When one comes to saving faith in Christ he is baptized by the Spirit and is placed, in Christ, into the body.

There was a second movement of the Holy Spirit on that day. In Acts 2:4 we read, "And they were all filled." The baptism of the Spirit has to do with *position,* but the moment we are placed in the body we are in a position for the filling of God's Spirit. The command comes to every believer, "Be filled with the Spirit" (Ephesians 5:18).

My heart rejoices in the blessing that came that day when, in answer to the prayer of the Lord Jesus, the Spirit came to baptize believers into the body, thus providing a relationship with our risen Lord that would make us adequate for every situation. From these great truths of realization, fulfillment and blessing, we see that Pentecost was—

A Day of Manifestation

A new order had begun in history. With it came the sound of rushing, mighty wind, and the appearance of tongues as of fire. God was getting the attention of men.

You cannot read Exodus 19 without being stirred. On this day when God gave the Law there was thunder, lightning, the sound of the trumpet; and Mt. Sinai was smoking. Why was this? God was doing a new thing in history. I have visited lovely Jewish synagogues from time to time and heard the Law read, but there was no thunder, no lightning, no trumpet. Why? At Sinai a new order was being established. The Law remained but the phenomenon passed. The same is true of Pentecost.

As we look at the book of Acts we see that the filling of the Spirit never stands alone. *It is always linked with a virtue.* God fills us, not that we may impress others, but that we may be a blessing to a needy world. The result of filling is communication, a divine enablement for spreading a message. The early believers, in the face of insurmountable difficulties, were bold to speak.

Another evidence of the Spirit's filling, one that I am confident made a terrific impact upon the society into which the church was thrust, was the fact they were a supremely happy lot. There are over twenty references to *joy* in the book of Acts. (This should say something to us today.) Moreover, the filling of the Spirit gave them good, common sense! Take a good look at Acts 6:1-7.

The filling of the Spirit gave the early Church power to live, to speak, to work, to pray, to triumph!

CHAPTER 3
Program for Action

I have always enjoyed museums. And there is a tug on my heart whenever I stand before an ancient, beautifully preserved car. I can almost hear it saying, "You would have enjoyed a day's journey with me." Strange as the Model "T" or the Chevrolet 490 appears, there are some basic things on those cars that have not changed. There are the wheels, different in style but still wheels; there is the motor, the transmission, the steering column. As time goes on, cars will still be built with these basic parts.

In a day when the ages were changing from law to grace, God dropped the church into the stream of history. The church was introduced with a divine origin, and was planned, patterned and perpetuated by the Christ who loved her and bought her (Ephesians 5:25). As we look in upon that early company of believers, it is possible for us to discern certain principles—truths that can be traced through the book of Acts, the Epistles and the history of the church. As we focus our attention on Acts 2:41-47 we see a pattern of what the church should be in the dispensation of God's grace.

When God, in His wisdom, placed me in my first pastorate, the circumstances were somewhat unusual. The doors of the church had been closed for nearly a year due to the community's lack of interest in spiritual things. I pried open the door of the church with a screwdriver, entered its dusty regions and rang the church bell for the whole town to hear. On the first Sunday the congregation consisted of seven elderly folk. As the days went by, and the congregation grew, I discovered that my classes in Pastoral Theology had not answered all the problems.

In our times together at the breakfast table, Mrs. Sugden and I read and reread the book of Acts. One truth gripped our hearts: *God's work would have to be done God's way if we were to have God's blessing.* As we read, there came a deepening conviction that the gates of Hell would be assaulted and God's program carried out only if certain principles were followed. Church growth and advancement would surely come as a result of following Scriptural guidelines.

I frequently find myself looking back across the years to those early days of ministry to find that God's intention and program did not change in the middle of the twentieth century. You must feel as I do that if the church of the twentieth century were to lay hold of the principles set forth in Acts, our fragmented and frustrated society would be startled.

W. H. Griffith Thomas has this to say in his *Outline Studies in Acts:* "The first of anything, be it specimen or illustration, is usually of great interest, as for example, the first book ever printed, or the first newspaper, or the first railroad engine or airplane. These verses in Acts are the record of the first Christian Church in its present organized form; and they contain the germ of everything else found in the New Testament concerning the Christian Community."

As I observe the happenings of today I am impressed with the statement in Acts 2:41, "And the same day there were added unto them about three thousand souls." Gaebelein, in *The Acts of the Apostles,* makes this interesting and valid observation: "We ask, added to what? Certainly to the company of believers, which by the baptism of the Holy Spirit had been formed into one body."

What abiding and unchanging truths are evident in the company who would "climb the steep ascent to heaven through peril, toil and pain"! W. Graham Scroggie states, "This passage cannot be read too often, and it should not be difficult to separate the local and temporary from the universal and abiding" (from *The Unfolding Drama of Redemption).*

Truth Relating to Admission

One thing comes through to us loud and clear as we reflect on Acts, chapter 2. *A man stood up to preach* (verse 11). It is always a great moment when a man heralds the gospel message, for this pleases the eternal God (I Corinthians 1:21). Heaven is astir when a man preaches. Peter's sermon had as its focal point a person—the Lord Jesus Christ (verses 22-36).

Wouldn't you be excited right now if you could push the button on your tape recorder and hear the moderator of the meeting announce, "Peter will now speak to us on the person of Christ"? We have in our libraries scores of books on Christology, but none can excel Peter's passioned address. Peter shows us Jesus Christ as (a) a man approved of God (Acts 2:22), (b) a man delivered by God (verse 23), (c) a man taken and crucified (verse 23), (d) a man loosed and raised (verse 24), (e) a man ascended to the Father (verse 33), and (f) a man keeping His word (verse 33).

This word proclaimed was gladly received, resulting in a regenerated membership in that original fellowship of believers. The passing centuries have not changed the original pattern. In fact, it would be a faith-building exercise to travel through the book of Acts and reflect upon the accomplishment of the Word of God. When Peter and John are given an opportunity to speak, they remind their hearers about the Prince of life who was delivered up (Acts 3:12-26). The result of their witness is set forth in Acts 4:4, "Howbeit many of them which heard the word believed; and the number of the men was about five thousand." And as you continue through Acts, don't pass by Acts 6:6,7; Acts 8:14; and Acts 11:1.

Isn't God trying to turn our attention to the truth that the work we desire to see carried out is accomplished only by the Word of God? Paul emphasizes this. He tells us that God's initial work in individual lives is the result of the ministry of God's Word: "So then faith cometh by hearing, and hearing by the word of God" (Romans 10:17).

The Spirit of God would not allow Peter to forget this truth. When he wrote his letter to "strengthen thy brethren" (Luke 22:32), he assured them that God's regenerative work can only be accomplished by the Word. "Being born again, not of corruptible seed, but of incorruptible, by the word of God, which liveth and abideth forever," he wrote in I Peter 1:23.

This truth was confirmed to me a few years ago when I was privileged to be in a series of campus meetings at Syracuse University. Each evening before the meeting I visited various fraternities on campus. At one house I noted especially keen interest among the men, shown by the many questions they asked. As I slipped away and walked alone on the beautiful campus I found myself wondering just what results might follow the meetings. A few years later I received a letter that taught me a great deal about results. The letter was from a young man studying for the ministry. He told me of a night on campus when he heard the Word of God and was saved. He said he was preparing for the ministry in answer to God's call to him. The seed sown that evening in the "frat" house had fallen on good soil, and I was reminded that *the Word of God does the work of God.*

Truth Relating to Practice

As you read Acts 2:41-46 over and over I am sure you are impressed with one word that is the key to the mightiness of God's movement in history. It is the word "together." If you had visited the early church on a Lord's Day morning you would have found people of different ages, different backgrounds, and different temperaments, but God had worked a miracle of grace in their lives. When they trusted Christ they were added to the church—but that's not all. They were added to each other. This gives not only the thought of nearness, but the wonder of belonging to each other. I have found—and I know you have—that one of the greatest problems in our society is the nagging problem of loneliness. The solution should be found in our belonging to Christ and to each other. John Fawcett's hymn, "Blest Be the Tie that

Binds," suggests:

We share our mutual woes,
Our mutual burdens bear;
And often for each other flows
The sympathizing tear.

Did you know that the word "saint" is never found in the singular in the New Testament? For the strengthening of our own lives and with a prayer for the local church, note how this unity was evidenced.

They were together in spiritual unity (Acts 2:42). Physical and spiritual growth both depend upon food. A skinny body usually indicates a lack of nourishment, and a thin soul always indicates a lack of spiritual nourishment. The early believers were developing well-developed souls, for they gave attention to the teaching of the apostles. They were dependent upon this teaching for truth concerning their new lives and the new work that God was doing. The Lord had promised them in John 14:26 and John 15:26 that direction would be given them so their teaching would be backed by the authority of Heaven.

Peter tells us that one of the evidences of life is appetite (I Peter 2:1-3). Then, lest his readers forget, his final word is "Grow in grace and in the knowledge of our Lord and Saviour, Jesus Christ" (II Peter 3:18). It is a delight to see those who have come to Christ making progress in their spiritual lives. We should never move beyond the desire expressed in the words of J. C. Lavater:

O Jesus Christ grow Thou in me
And all things else recede:
My heart be daily nearer thee;
From sin be daily freed.
Make this poor self grow less and less,
Be Thou my life, my aim,
O make me daily through Thy grace
More meet to bear Thy name.

They were together in fellowship (Acts 2:42). Frequently we sing songs whose meanings are enriched with passing years. For example, "What a fellowship, what a joy divine, leaning on the everlasting arms" speaks profoundly of this blessing of life. It would be good to spend time in reflection on various aspects of fellowship: (a) fellowship with God the Father (I John 1:3), (b) fellowship with the Son (I Corinthians 1:9), (c) fellowship with the Holy Spirit (Philippians 2:1), (d) fellowship in friendship (I John 1:7), (e) fellowship in giving (II Corinthians 8:4), (f) fellowship in the gospel (Philippians 1:5).

Thomas Walker has an excellent word in his commentary on this subject: "The word [*fellowship*] is a comprehensive one in the New Testament, being used not only of brotherly association, but also of joint participation in spiritual blessings and of the communication or distribution of earthly goods" (from *Acts of the Apostles*).

They were together in the breaking of bread (Acts 2:42). Thomas Lindsay in his work, *Acts of the Apostles,* makes this brief comment, "'Breaking of bread' is the earliest New Testament phrase for the Lord's Supper."

Isn't it an unspeakable privilege to gather together for this memorial feast and to realize that you are joining hands with the saints of the Church Age in a distinctive meal?—a meal that looks back to Calvary where Jesus died for us, up to the throne where He lives for us, and forward to the day when He will come for us!

They were together in prayer (verse 42). It is an exciting experience to recapture the wonder of prayer and its power as set forth in this inspired portrait of the march of the church. Prayer solved problems and secured leaders (Acts 1:24-26). Prayer brought them privilege (Acts 2:1-11). Prayer gave ability to communicate the message (Acts 4:29-31). Prayer brought vision (Acts 10:9). Prayer brought deliverance to men (Acts 12:5-16). Prayer thrust forth workers (Acts 13:1-3). Prayer made their witness effective (Acts 16:25). Prayer secured guidance (Acts 22:17,18).

We ought to pray that God would restore to the church a renewed desire for this spiritual exercise, remembering that "Prayer is the mightiest force that man can wield, a power to which omnipotence doth yield."

Truth Relating to Progress

When you read the book of Acts you are

startled at the growth of the church (Acts 2:47). The three thousand converted at Pentecost soon became five thousand. The Word of God increased and a "great company of the priests were obedient to the faith" (Acts 6:7). What was the secret of this mighty movement of God? The twofold answer offers practical help for today's church:

God was doing the unusual. In that day signs and wonders were wrought by the apostles. Although the apostolic office has ceased, God is still alive and He is yet the God of miracles. The greatest wonder in this day is the miracle of the *new birth* wrought by the preaching of the Word of God.

God gave the church favor with the people. There was a quality of life among the early Christians that arrested a watching world, aroused their curiosity and attracted them to Christ. It was characteristic of the times that God was doing great things. His "great power" and "great grace" were clearly evident (Acts 4:33).

The church today—yours and mine—can be similarly blessed of God. The challenge is before us. Let's meet the challenge, and give credence to the song:

> *Like a mighty army*
> *Moves the church of God;*
> *Brothers, we are treading*
> *Where the saints have trod.*

CHAPTER 4
Assault through Authority

*T*he buzzer on my desk rang to announce that I had a visitor. A gentleman of some dignity stepped through the door, and I was aware that here was an unusual man. He did something I am sure he had done many times, for it came smoothly and automatically. With a left hook he scraped his body, hit his inside pocket, and flipped open a little leather case. As it opened I saw his picture, his name and his position. Then having shown me his credentials he reached out his hand, told me his name and announced, "I have come today to talk about one of the young men in your congregation whom we are considering for a responsible position in our government.

Would you be willing to answer some questions about him?"

When he pulled the list of questions out of his slim attache case I anticipated spending the remainder of the day with him. After he had asked question after question, he finally ended his interview by asking, "Would you feel that our country would be safe in the hands of this young man?" I assured him it would, so he thanked me and left.

This man came to me with credentials. Not everyone who comes to my office feels the need to prove his identity, for of course not everyone comes as a representative of the Federal Government.

If the gates of the enemy of the church are to be assaulted, spiritual battles won and territory conquered, it must be through men who carry the *credentials of Heaven.*

Men of Authority

The book of Acts has scarcely opened its inviting doors to us before we meet a company of men called "apostles." They greet us in Acts 1:2, where we learn that Christ "through the Holy Ghost, had given commandments unto the apostles whom he had chosen." These divinely chosen men confront us at every turn. When one of their company defaults, the Lord in answer to prayer directs them to the man who will fill his place. When the day of Pentecost comes in its fullness they are there, and are baptized into one body. The first message to be proclaimed is heralded by an apostle.

Now let's go back to that eventful day of the apostolic band's inception. The Lord Jesus has climbed a mountain, and there on the mountaintop He sees the church as it will be throughout history. The scene in Mark's Gospel is rich with significance: "And he goeth up into a mountain, and calleth unto him whom he would: and they came unto him. And he ordained twelve, that they should be with him, and that he might send them forth to preach" (Mark 3:13,14).

Graham Scroggie in his volume, *Mark,* has this to say about that event: "Those twelve men were destined to make history. Here, the more we think the more we shall wonder. But why twelve? No doubt the number was determined by the tribes of Israel, and together they appear in the final Apocalypse, in the four and twenty elders, and in the twelve gates, and twelve foundations of the Holy City (Revelation 4:4; 21:12,14)."

In the apostolic band there was represented every sort of personality under Heaven. We find a whole world in those apostles. Perhaps the Lord chose the whole world in the twelve so that none of us could presume that we had been left out of His plan.

Just what was significant about these twelve men? The apostles were present during our Lord's ministry. They were at Jordan when He was baptized by John. They were present at the cross. They stood breathless at the empty tomb. As though drawn by a mighty magnet, they assembled on the day of Pentecost when the Spirit came in answer to the Lord's prayer (John 14:16; Acts 2:33). They became the foundation stones for the mighty structure that would be built in fulfillment of our Lord's word to Peter in Matthew 16:18. We must not forget what Paul said in Ephesians 4:11,12: "And he gave some, apostles; and some, prophets; and some, evangelists; and some, pastors and teachers; For the perfecting of the saints, for the work of the ministry, for the edifying of the body of Christ."

The gifts to the church from the ascended Christ provided for its foundation—apostles and prophets; provided for its extension—evangelists; and provided for its continuance—pastors and teachers. Apostles and prophets, listed at the beginning, had to do with the foundation.

In God's good providence I have been privileged to be associated with my present church for twenty-three years. Through these years a number of building projects have been accomplished. With joy the congregation watched the laying of the foundations. Each was laid only once. The foundations were not laid over and over again. Upon those well-placed and well-poured foundations superstructures have been built.

Paul reminds the believers at Ephesus of the truth of this in Ephesians 2:19,20: "Now therefore ye are no more strangers and foreigners, but fellowcitizens with the saints, and of the household of God; And are built upon the foundation of the apostles and prophets, Jesus Christ himself being the chief corner stone."

It is of the utmost importance that we spend time with the apostles in order to understand their ministry and its relation to the church today, for *their ministry was foundational.* With the coming of a new age those who ministered found it necessary to carry credentials with them. What were these credentials that the apostles carried?

As you read Paul's second letter to the Corinthians you find that his apostleship was being questioned in chapters eleven and twelve. The pressure that was brought upon him compelled him to inform them (and he even boasted a bit about it) that he was an authentic messenger of God. He said, "Truly the signs of an apostle were wrought among you in all patience, in signs, and wonders, and mighty deeds" (II Corinthians 12:12).

The Signs of an Apostle

If the believers at Corinth were reminded that the signs of an apostle had been evidenced in their midst, then the nature of these signs must have been common knowledge.

Let's go back to the original sending forth of the twelve in Matthew 10. The Lord Jesus gave them "power against unclean spirits, to cast them out, and to heal all manner of sickness and all manner of disease" (verse 1). He admonished them, "Heal the sick, cleanse the lepers, raise the dead, cast out devils" (verse 8). After the Lord Jesus had risen from the dead, and before He returned to be seated on His Father's throne, He again mentioned the disciples' power (Mark 16:17,18).

One thing is inescapable: the ministry of the apostles involved signs. Frequently we find linked with *signs* two other words: *miracles* and *wonders*. This was true on the day of Pentecost, for "fear came upon every soul: and many wonders and signs were done by the apostles" (Acts 2:43). The early church prayed, in an hour of crisis, that the Lord would stretch forth His hand "to heal; and that signs and wonders might be done in the name of thy holy child Jesus" (Acts 4:30).

Calvin has a great word on this. "Paul calls them signs, because they are not empty shows, but are appointed for the instruction of mankind; wonders, because they ought by their novelty, to arouse men and strike them with astonishment; and mighty deeds, because they are more signal tokens of divine power than what we behold in the ordinary course of nature" (from the *Tyndale New Testament Commentaries*).

Purpose of Signs

I am impressed with the fact that whenever God begins a new work in His sovereign purpose He accentuates it with the unusual. When He gave the law there were thunders and lightnings, the sound of a trumpet and the voice of God, "and the whole mount quaked greatly" (Exodus 19:18). From that day to this the law has been read ten thousand times ten thousand, but there has been no thunder, no lightning, no earthquake. This *did* happen when the law was introduced, for God was doing something new and He validated it with signs.

Why did God give to the apostles signs, wonders, miracles? *To validate the message.*

In the *New International Commentary of the New Testament* Hodge says, "The signs of an apostle were the insignia of the apostleship. These signs were confirmatory of the apostolic work and word, and therefore of the authenticity of the apostles' mission."

The *signs* of the apostles were their identification cards. They had no New Testament Scriptures to point to, so when someone charged, "You are a fake!" or "You're not for real," the validity of their position was proved by a miracle.

We must also recognize that they not only performed miracles to authenticate the message, but they also performed miracles because they were working with Jewish people. Paul wrote in I Corinthians 1:21,22: "For after that in the wisdom of God the world by wisdom knew not God, it pleased God by the foolishness of preaching to save them that believe. For the Jews require a sign...." You cannot escape the fact that the first ten chapters of the book of Acts are basically about Jews. The Jews said, "Prove it," and the answer was, "All right, here is a sign."

You will remember that there are three

chapters in Acts where the gift of tongues was in evidence. Paul, in I Corinthians 14:22, states tersely, "tongues are for a sign." They were given to validate, to confirm. In Acts 2 they were for the world outside. In Acts 10 they were to convince Peter and the men accompanying him that God had broken down the wall of partition between Jews and Gentiles and that the Gentiles had been received by Him. Imagine the scene as we visualize this dramatic event in Acts 10:44,45. "While Peter yet spake these words, the Holy Ghost fell on all them who heard the word. And they of the circumcision which believed were astonished, as many as came with Peter, because that on the Gentiles also was poured out the gift of the Holy Ghost."

When we stop at Ephesus with Paul, we find a Jewish company who had not heard that their faith was to rest in Jesus Christ (Acts 19:4). They believed, and a sign was given to validate the work that had been accomplished.

The Cessation of Signs

When Paul confronted the Corinthian Church with evidences of his apostleship, he reminded them that he was not inferior to others. "In nothing am I behind the very chiefest apostles, though I be nothing" (II Corinthians 12:11). The proof of his position had been confirmed by his having wrought "the signs of an apostle" (verse 12). He did not say, "the signs of a Christian," or "the signs of a believer," but the signs of one who had been duly chosen as a part of the church's foundation.

George T. Purves, onetime Professor of New Testament at Princeton Theological Seminary, wrote an informative book on the apostolic age. He observed "An apostle must have been a disciple of Jesus through His ministry from the close of that of the Baptist. This evidently assumes that he was to teach Christ's whole message, life and work, which alone made the resurrection of unique importance....To the world they were the official witnesses of the resurrection, to the church its official instructors and overseers" (from *The Apostolic Age*).

Based on the special nature and qualifications of the apostolic office we may conclude that there are no apostles today. The apostolic band was not a self-perpetuating board. With the death of apostles the apostolic office ceased. With its cessation the signs of an apostle were no longer essential.

The gradual decline of signs is clearly seen in the book of Acts. In the opening chapters prison doors miraculously pop open often, but when the curtain falls at its close Paul is still confined in jail.

W. Graham Scroggie, in *The Baptism of the Spirit and Speaking in Tongues,* says, "The miracles of the apostolic age, which served during their period as signs, gradually ceased to be displayed, the need for them having been superceded; and that in the present age sensuous evidences have given place to spiritual evidences."

Furthermore, in *Speaking in Tongues,* Stolee observes, "This gift served its purpose as a sign from God in the Church's childhood."

Gromacki, in his excellent book, *The Modern Tongues Movement,* affirms, "In the post-apostolic era, speaking in tongues ceased as a normal activity of the believers."

About the cessation of apostolic signs, Dr. H. A. Ironside has this to say in his commentary, *First Epistle to the Corinthians,* "We are not told of any special limit, so far as time is concerned, yet we know both from Scripture and Church History that most of the so-called miraculous gifts passed away shortly after the Bible was complete."

The foundation of the church having been laid, she now moves forward to her greatest hour, the time of her consummation. Paul wrote about Christ's ultimate goal for the church in Ephesians 5:27, "That he might present it to himself a glorious church, not having spot, or wrinkle, or any such thing; but that it should be holy and without blemish." While we contemplate that day, we are ambassadors of Heaven, and as such we move with all the authority of the throne of God. Our sole credential for this awesome responsibility is the unchanging, eternal Word of the living God. Emotions, experiences, and feelings may fluctuate, but our message is validated by a "thus saith the Lord." Song writer William How captured the

truth of this and gave to us one of our choice
hymns:

> *O Word of God incarnate,*
> *O wisdom from on high,*
> *O Truth unchanged, unchanging,*
> *O light of our dark sky:*
> *We praise thee for the radiance*
> *That from the hallowed page,*
> *A lantern to our footsteps,*
> *Shines on from age to age."*

CHAPTER 5

ACTION THROUGH ORGANIZATION

*T*he phone on my desk rang abruptly.

"There's another problem," I told myself. As I lifted the receiver I heard a sob.

"Pastor, why are all these things happening to our family? We move from one crisis to another. Why?"

In this day when the watchword is "escape" we need to remember that problems and troubles are the tools by which God fashions us for better things. It is good for us to learn the lesson expressed by the psalmist: "Before I was afflicted I went astray: but now have I kept thy word....It is good for me that I have been afflicted; that I might learn thy statutes" (Psalm 119:67,71).

Some time ago I stood in the very spot

where Samuel Rutherford ministered the Word of God to his congregation. Few men experienced such troubles as he experienced them. On one occasion he testified, "Why should I tremble at the plough of my Lord, that maketh deep furrows on my soul? I know He is no idle husbandman. He purposeth a crop."

In hours of sheer desperation the God of Heaven strengthens us as we realize that He is using varied experiences to shape us into useful instruments.

One day I received a letter from a young man who was passing through severe trials in the war in Viet Nam. There was no word of complaint or criticism. As I read the letter I found the reason for his healthy outlook in the triumphant words, "God is doing a great work in my life during these days."

Frequently along roadways our attention is called to flashing lights and the sign, *Men at Work*. In Philippians 2:13 we are reminded that God has placed on our lives a "sign" which says, "It is God which worketh in you." Staggering, isn't it? The God who flung out creation is this very moment at work in us. The result of this work is threefold: humility (Philippians 2:5-8), contentment (Philippians 2:14), and testimony (Philippians 2:15).

Only the indwelling Spirit of God could do such a mighty work of humbling us, sweetening us, and making us a light in a dark and squalid place. You may have noticed in your study of God's Word that the Epistles frequently present the work of God in individual lives, whereas the book of Acts is the authentic account of the work of God in the collective group. God is not only working in us as individuals, but He is at work in the local, visible church of which I am a vital part.

The early company of believers was marked by growth. This advance can be traced, in the opening chapters of Acts, to the fact that the believers had no communication problem. They took advantage of every opportunity to set forth the majesty of Jesus Christ and His power to salvage life. When they were brought before the authorities of Jerusalem and questioned, they climaxed their testimony by affirming, "Neither is there salvation in any other: for there is none other name under heaven given among men, whereby we must be saved" (Acts 4:12).

That a divine constraint rested upon the company of believers is evidenced in their words to a hostile audience: "We cannot but speak the things which we have seen and heard" (Acts 4:20).

Many books have been written on the subject of church advancement and growth, but it is doubtful that the method of the early church can be improved upon. "And with great power gave the apostles witness of the resurrection of the Lord Jesus: and great grace was upon them all" (Acts 4:33). There needs to be recaptured in our assemblies the "great power" that manifested itself in "great grace." Then we will find our churches in the midst of "great growth."

But times of expansion can become times of problem. We are not surprised when we look in upon this vital company to hear murmuring about the way the welfare system was being handled (Acts 6:1). "Murmuring" is an interesting word. It means *to mutter, to grumble, to say anything in an undertone*. Can you believe that the grumbling came because of "food stamps"?

Let us survey what happened with a desire for God to apply truth to our hearts.

There Are Blessings That Produce Problems

We've all found this to be true. In fact, most of us find that blessing is the road over which so many of our troubles travel. The little baby who comes to our home to bless us brings with him built-in troubles for our hearts. The growth in our business catapults upon us pressures that we never dreamed of. Pastors with large congregations look back to the day when the flock was small with the realization that the blessing of growth has brought attendant problems.

Great blessing had come to the early church. They believed heartily in the promise given by their Lord: "He that goeth forth and weepeth, bearing precious seed, shall doubtless come again with rejoicing, bringing his sheaves with him" (Psalm 126:6). Lenski, in his commentary, *Acts of the Apostles,* observes the early church and reminds us of its rapidly increasing size. He writes: "It has been conservatively estimated that at this time the total number of the disciples was between twenty and twenty-five thousand."

This is exactly what God has intended the church to do—grow. There are folk who feel that if the church is kept small it will not have problems. We need to be reminded that "smallness *is* a problem." The Galatian churches were small and they ended up back-biting. Growth is the law of God in both the physical and the spiritual realms. The healthy church is the growing church. This simply means that every church should seek to reach her potential. It has been my privilege to observe churches in farming communities and small towns achieving an increasing, expanding ministry as they sought to reach their potential.

If growth follows sowing—and it does for this is the rule of God—be prepared for problems. Increased blessings always produce problems. If we embrace all that God has embraced, there will be all kinds of folk in our congregation.

Satan has tried to destroy the church with persecution (Acts 4:1-17) and with deception (Acts 5:1-11), but his plans have been thwarted. Now he seeks to array believer against believer with dissension, which can be fatal. The Hebrews were in the majority, and the Greeks cried, "We're neglected! You don't pay any attention to us!" The same thing could happen today.

We have found that the blessings given so freely of God may create problems. We now see that—

The Blessings Reveal a Peril

Nineteen hundred plus years have passed, but every church that seeks to do a work for God still faces the peril that leaped upon the infant assembly. The peril is twofold. First, the physical may become more important than the spiritual, and the secular more important than the sacred. How many churches do you know that have fragmented on this issue? Even the early church met with this problem, as is shown in Acts 6:1,2. There is nothing wrong with food, with eating, with church fellowship, but if the physical becomes more important than the spiritual, we are in real danger.

Secondly, we may find ourselves wasting first-rate energies on second-rate causes. It is tragic to discover that those who have been called to spiritual service end up preparing luncheons rather than dispensing the Bread of Life. Note the evidence of God's guidance in the infant church. They did not shun the physical, the material; they simply gave God priority. In so doing they were obedient to the word spoken by the Lord Jesus in Matthew 6:33: "But seek ye first the kingdom of God, and his righteousness; and all these things shall be added unto you."

We now examine an aspect of the church for which we can be grateful. It is—

The Blessing That Presented a Need

If there is need to care for the temporal as well as the spiritual, and if God has ordained balance between secular and sacred, then it is evident that we need *organization*. Everything that we see in creation is eloquent in affirming that God is a God of order. The sun that lights our days, the moon that lights our nights, the changing seasons, impress us with the fact that order is important to God. When Paul sought to correct the abuses that had crept into the Corinthian Church, he exhorted, "Let all things be done decently and in order" (I Corinthians 14:40).

God called to the young congregation of believers in Jerusalem to arrange a meeting of the assembly in order to choose men to serve as deacons (Acts 6:3). We are impressed that the democratic ideal was practiced by the early church. The whole church was invited to partake in the choice of suitable men to serve as deacons. Peter did not make the decision. Nor did the rest of the apostles. All members were privileged to share in this solemn business of choosing suitable men to carry on God's business.

Let's look in upon this meeting that was to set the pattern for the work of the church through the centuries. It was a meeting bathed in prayer (Acts 6:6). The work of God must be carried on by men who are qualified for such ministry.

We must not pass lightly by the marks of the men who were chosen to serve. We learn from these what our deacons must be. They must be men of honest report (verse 3), in the community as well as in the church. They must be men full of the Holy Ghost (verse 3).

(A Spirit-filled man is one whose life manifests the fruit of the Spirit—Galatians 5:22,23.) They must be men full of wisdom (verse 3). This is tremendous, for the word *wisdom* literally means *good practical sense.* Think of having men on the board of deacons with good common sense. What a joy to the heart of a pastor, for how important it is to be practical! Finally, they must be men full of faith (verse 5). It is imperative that men in God's work know the deep secret of trusting the living God. Hebrews, chapter eleven, gives to us something of the magnitude of faith's power and faith's accomplishments. May this faith and all that it brings be ours.

The time finally came that would reveal whether or not the church would split. The ballots had been prepared. The ushers had passed them to the members, and it was time to count the votes. We find that—

The Blessing Demonstrated God's Grace

The need that had arisen furnished a backdrop for God to show how mightily He works in the lives of men. If there is any hour in the life of the local chruch when there is need for a manifestation of the grace of God, it's in the monthly or annual business meeting. It is always good to remember that Heaven is concerned about such meetings, and that angels are always in attendance to learn as they behold the wisdom of God reflected in "I support" or "I object." This certainly is the truth conveyed to the church at

Ephesus in Ephesians 3:10: "To the intent that now unto the principalities and powers in heavenly places might be known by the church the manifold wisdom of God."

Pellegrin, in his *Epistle to the Ephesians,* sees in this a great picture. "The church is God's army being watched by angels who are unable to fathom God's wish for us; the church is a class room in which angels learn their lessons."

How much is at stake on earth and in Heaven when the business of God is being conducted! What did the angels see as they looked in upon the business meeting that night at the First Church? They saw a miracle of grace displayed through human personality. They were astounded as they witnessed a principally Hebrew congregation elect seven Greeks.

Thomas Walker gives a valuable observation about this in his commentary on Acts. "We notice that the names of the seven all are Greek, not Hebrew, and we may fairly conclude that all alike were chosen from the Hellenistic party. If so, the election marks the triumph of the spirit of love and liberality, for they were clearly chosen by the united suffrage of the whole church. All ground for discontent on the part of the Grecian Jews was thus removed in the most magnanimous manner possible."

What was the result of this demonstration of God's grace and love in the life of the early church? One word tells the story: *advance.* God's guidance, demonstrated in the lives of those who comprised the early church, made a tremendous impact upon the world. "And the word of God increased; and the number of the disciples multiplied in Jerusalem greatly; and a great company of the priests were obedient to the faith" (Acts 6:7).

How wonderful it would be if such an entry could be made in the diary of every church. Remember, church organization under God's direction will bring glorious victories.

CHAPTER 6

Vision for Action

When Joyce Kilmer looked out upon God's creation he wrote:

I think that I shall never see
A poem as lovely as a tree.
A tree whose hungry mouth is pressed
Against the earth's sweet flowing breast;
A tree that looks at God all day
And lifts her leafy arms to pray;
A tree that may in summer wear
A nest of robins in her hair;
Upon whose bosom snow has lain;
Who intimately lives with rain.
Poems are made by fools like me,
But only God can make a tree.

—from Favorite Poems Old and New

Sometimes, when I read this poem, I can almost imagine that Kilmer drove north across the lovely state of Michigan, where I pastor, and stopped to spend an hour in Hartwick Pines. Not long ago I walked through this tremendous forest and found myself wondering just how it came to be. What or who was responsible for planting that first seed? Was the winged seed carried by a strong wind from its home to a place far from the parent tree? Or did an Indian carry it on the sole of his moccasin from its original place to where it buried itself in the warm soil and started to grow?

We have in our possession the Word of God, a Word which is forever settled in Heaven (Psalm 119:89). Of the twenty-seven books that form our New Testament, over half of them were penned by a chosen human instrument named Paul. It was Paul who announced to the Jews in Antioch of Pisidia that "through [Christ] is preached unto you the forgiveness of sins: And by him all that believe are justified from all things, from which ye could not be justified by the law of Moses" (Acts 13:38,39). It was Paul who carried the gospel to Europe, established a beachhead in a hostile pagan world, and planted the blood-stained banner of the cross. Someone has said that by every literary, theological and spiritual standard, he was *the* towering figure of church history. Purves, in his excellent book *The Apostolic Age,* brings Paul before us with these words, "Saul of Tarsus possessed a remarkable personality. He was one of those intense natures to whom truth and duty are so commanding as to be at once transmuted into life. His mental aptitudes were also singularly varied, and in every direction almost equally vigorous. He was a keen thinker. To him a principle became at once fruitful of a system, so that he followed an idea to its logical implications.Yet he had a strongly emotional temperament. He was capable of tremendous passion, and he always felt the full reality of what he enjoyed or suffered."

Looking in upon this figure as he moved from Tarsus to Jerusalem to continue his study, we find ourselves asking, "How will God drop the seed into the soil of his soul to produce a mighty harvest? What means will He use?"

We would like to trace the working of God that changed this man's life from *sinner* to *saint,* from Saul to Paul, and that made him the courageous carrier of eternal truth. There was an hour when he saw something—an hour when truth arrested, captured and transformed him.

Witnesses jammed the court as the Council of Seventy leaned forward intently. A young man with the face of an angel was expounding Israel's history. As Saul and the rest of the Council listened he could not miss the fact that here was a man who knew the Scriptures, believed the Scriptures, preached the Scriptures, and applied the Scriptures. Later on, when the living Christ met Saul upon his return from Damascus to Jerusalem, Saul explained to the Lord how his part in this violent scene had been a goad to prod him. Hear his own witness of this recorded in Acts 22:19, 20: "And I said, Lord, they know that I imprisoned and beat in every synagogue those that believed on thee: And when the blood of thy martyr Stephen was shed, I also was standing by, and consenting unto his death, and kept the raiment of them that slew him."

How much is revealed by the word, *consenting*. It means "to take pleasure in." Saul watched the clothes that were heaped at his feet while his rebellious heart enjoyed what was taking place before him. Later Paul recounted this event for the benefit of King Agrippa, before whom he stood as a prisoner. He acknowledged: "I verily thought with myself, that I ought to do many things contrary to the name of Jesus of Nazareth" (Acts 26:9). From that hour came truths that seized Saul and prepared the soil of his soul for the seed that would fall and later produce a crop that has never yet been fully harvested. What was it that made him bend low over the clothes that were heaped on the ground before him? What was it that he could not shake from his troubled mind?—It was the dauntless testimony of a believer who lived by the power of the risen Christ.

Is it possible that believers today can manifest in these turbulent hours the same things that shone through the life of Stephen? If the church could emulate such powerful testimony, no doubt we would have more force in our world that scrutinizes us so closely.

The Power of the Holy Spirit

Stephen had delivered his message without the encouragement of a friendly face or an approving nod from his audience. With boldness he declared to the Sanhedrin truths that tore their hearts: "Ye stiffnecked and uncircumcised in heart and ears, ye do always resist the Holy Ghost: as your fathers did, so do ye. Which of the prophets have not your fathers persecuted? and they have slain them which shewed before of the coming of the Just One; of whom ye have been now the betrayers and murderers: Who have received the law by the disposition of angels, and have not kept it" (Acts 7:51-53). Following an awesome silence they gnashed on him, "But he, being full of the Holy Ghost, looked up stedfastly into heaven, and saw the glory of God, and Jesus standing on the right hand of God" (Acts 7:55).

Saul saw a man filled with the Spirit of God. Before his eyes stood a man with the credentials of Heaven. Later when Paul penned his letter to the believers at Ephesus, he must have recalled this scene as he encouraged them to "be filled with the Spirit" (Ephesians 5:18).

Stephen, filled with the Spirit, looked up stedfastly. In this day marked by the fragmentation of churches on the subject of the filling with the Holy Spirit, it is of the utmost importance to realize what the fullness of the Spirit is. The Greek word for "stedfastly" in

Acts 7:55 is also used for "fastening" in Acts 3:4 where it is recorded that Peter was fastening his eyes upon a lame man. In Acts 3:12 it is "earnestly."

If we are to survive in this desperate day, we, like Stephen, need to fasten our eyes on Christ. David learned this lesson when King Saul was threatening him daily. He wrote, "I have set the Lord always before me: because he is at my right hand. I shall not be moved" (Psalm 16:8). And when the Hebrew Christians were living under threat of violence, the eloquent writer urged, "Run the race . . . . Looking unto Jesus" (Hebrews 12:1,2).

When the Holy Spirit fills a believer, we may be sure that he focuses that believer's attention on Jesus Christ. The Spirit-filled believer doesn't snoop around as a "people watcher."

As Saul saw Stephen's stedfastness in his hour of crisis, he was aware of—

The Reality of the Invisible World

Saul had never been unaware of that world. At his mother's knee and in his father's house he had listened to the reading of the Old Testament Scriptures. The world of angelic hosts was familiar to him. But suddenly he was faced with a man who was actually in touch with that invisible world. Its door was open to him. Saul could not miss the wonder of all that was happening. It was not so much the fact that here was a man who saw

Heaven, but that Heaven saw him and was moved in his behalf.

The book of Genesis furnishes us with a similar phenomenon. As Jacob found himself pursued by those who sought to destroy him, he was made aware of invisible forces of Heaven that ministered to his needs. He saw "a ladder set up on the earth, and the top of it reached to heaven: and behold the angels of God ascending and descending on it" (Genesis 28:12). How startling to realize that the angels are here with us and are actively engaged in the events of our lives. Later in Jacob's life when circumstances again were harsh, the citizens of the invisible world met him to put courage in his heart (Genesis 32:1).

It would be easy to quietly place this truth on the shelf labeled *Not for today* if the Bible did not speak of "ministering spirits, sent forth to minister for them who shall be heirs of salvation" (Hebrews 1:14). The word "salvation" in the Epistle to the Hebrews refers to the completion and fulfillment of God's work in our behalf. Angels minister to us until God has completed the good work He began in us. What strength and courage is ours when we remember that God has said, "I will never leave thee, nor forsake thee. So that we may boldly say, The Lord is my helper, and I will not fear what man shall do unto me" (Hebrews 13:5,6).

Saul saw in Stephen a man full of the Holy Spirit, a man aware of an open Heaven. But the curtain had not yet dropped on the scene, for he was also made aware of—

The Sufficiency of God's Grace

When Stephen cried out, "I see the heavens opened and Jesus standing," the Council of Seventy went wild. Its members turned into an infuriated mob. They shouted, stopped their ears, and with one accord advanced upon him with the powers of Hell.

Have you read *Fox's Book of Martyrs* lately? Is it your habit to keep clippings from news media on the sufferings presently inflicted on Christians in the Communist world? Has it ever occurred to you what would happen if it were *your* lot to pass through hours of severe testing? God allowed His people to pass through trials to give *us* encouragement in similar situations.

I am sure there are hours when it would be easier to die than to live. For such times Stephen steps before us. Look heavenward with him. What did he see? He saw Jesus *standing*. When you read the Epistle to the Hebrews you find that the Lord Jesus is *seated* at the right hand of God. Four times we see Him *seated* in the place of authority (Hebrews 1:3; 8:1; 10:12; 12:2). But as Stephen looked up through the open door of Heaven, he saw Jesus *standing*. How wonderful! The believer, moving through violent scenes on earth, is "in Christ." What touches us touches Him. Saul found this to be true on the road to Damascus when he heard the Lord Jesus demand, "Saul, Saul, why persecutest thou me? And he said, Who art thou, Lord? And the Lord said, I am Jesus whom thou persecutest:

it is hard for thee to kick against the pricks" (Acts 9:4,5). Up to that moment Saul knew nothing of the great truth of Christ's identification with the believers. No doubt he began to learn of it in that memorable Damascus Road transaction.

The risen, seated Christ was aware of Stephen's crisis. He saw Stephen and He stood up! It is evident that Christ stood to strengthen Stephen. This is one aspect of His great work as High Priest. He has invited us to "come boldly unto the throne of grace, that we may obtain mercy, and find grace to help in time of need" (Hebrews 4:16).

"Grace" in this context has to do with the strength that God has made available for us. When Paul asked relief from his thorn in the flesh, the Lord encouraged: "My grace is sufficient for thee: for my strength is made perfect in weakness." Paul's heart responded, "Most gladly therefore will I rather glory in my infirmities, that the power of Christ may rest upon me" (II Corinthians 12:9). He practiced what he had witnessed when Stephen was assaulted, and found strength for his hour of need. We, too, hear our Lord say,

> *When through fiery trials*
> *Thy pathway shall lie,*
> *My grace, all-sufficient,*
> *Shall be thy supply;*
> *The flames shall not hurt thee,*
> *I only design*
> *Thy dross to consume,*
> *And thy gold to refine.*

Our great High Priest stood to strengthen, but He also stood to welcome the one who was valiant in battle. Heaven was astir at the contest between the forces of Hell and Heaven. Divinely strengthened by the sufficient grace of Christ, Stephen prayed, "Lay not this sin to their charge" (Acts 7:60). As Paul heard this, the hard ground of his heart was being prepared for the seed that already had begun to fall.

On one occasion Joseph Parker heralded the greatness of the might of God in behalf of His people. Someone in the audience cried out, "Strength, did you say? What did He do for Stephen when they stoned him?" With his thunderous voice Parker cried back, "He gave him strength to pray for them—and that's victory!"

The Majesty of the Believer's Death

Death is inescapable. It is an appointment that we will all keep if the Lord does not return before that hour (Hebrews 9:27). Death and life, said Job, come from His hand (Job 1:21), "seeing [man's] days are determined, the number of his months are with thee, thou hast appointed his bounds that he cannot pass" (Job 14:5). For that appointed hour we possess the adequate grace of God. A Christian's death is a triumph, and it is precious in the sight of the Lord (Psalm 116:15).

Take another look at Stephen. Stones beat upon his body, but he "fell asleep." He stepped into the presence of his waiting Lord, but his *body* fell asleep. We should desire that God will teach us the truths he taught Saul through Stephen's death. Then others, through our ministry, may find the seed of God implanted in their lives.

CHAPTER 7

Getting Past the Wall

*I*n the year 214 B.C. one of the greatest engineering feats in history was under construction in China. Small sections of the barrier were probably already in existence by that year, but during Shih Huang Ti's reign alone, 470 miles of wall were built, and it is said that almost every third man throughout the empire was drafted for the undertaking. The wall averages twenty feet in height and is built of earth with a facing of brick and granite. A fifteen-foot roadway runs along the top where fortified square watch towers once carried beacon fires to flash warnings of disaster or to arouse the countryside.

When completed, the wall ran for 1400 miles over rugged mountains, down deep valleys, across meandering rivers. The Great Wall served as a strong defense against invasion and played an important part in the nation's life. In his *A Study of History* Arnold

Toynbee states: "The Great Wall of China proves on analysis, to be a lateral highway skirting the outmost verge of an empire's domain."

But great as this wall was, it could not compare with the wall that had been under construction for over 1500 years. That wall, although invisible, had separated Jew and Gentile through the centuries. Now, however, the early Christian church was assaulting this wall by telling men that God, in His sovereign purpose, was going to embrace all men.

On one occasion after His resurrection the disciples heard the Lord say, "Thus it is written, and thus it behoved Christ to suffer, and to rise from the dead the third day: And that repentance and remission of sins should be preached in his name among all nations, beginning at Jerusalem" (Luke 24:46,47).

When Peter, who heard this word from the risen Christ, preached on the day of Pentecost, he referred to the Holy Spirit's work as leaping the barriers that had always separated men. "For the promise is unto you, and to your children, and to all that are afar off, even as many as the Lord, our God shall call" (Acts 2:39) he announced.

Some years later when Paul penned his Epistle to the Ephesians, he saw that wall as fallen. He explained: "For he is our peace, who hath made both one, and hath broken down the middle wall of partition between us" (Ephesians 2:14).

We need to remind ourselves again and again that the partition that stood between

Jew and Gentile was no "man of straw." We get some concept of the problem's magnitude from what the historian Josephus said about this great barrier in *The Wars of the Jews*: "When you go through these first cloisters unto the second court of the Temple, there was a partition made of stone all round, whose height was three cubits. Its construction was very elegant; upon it stood pillars at equal distances from one another, declaring the law of purity, some in Greek and some in Roman letters that no foreigner should go inside the Sanctuary." He spoke again of this wall in *The Antiquities of the Jews* as he described the second court of the Temple: "This was encompassed by a stone wall for a partition, with an inscription which forbade any foreigner to go in under pain of death."

How would God break down this wall that kept men out through fear of death? What could God do to break down the wall between Jew and Gentile, pictured in the wall of the Temple that said, "Keep out"?

We look in upon a dramatic scene in Acts 10 to find the secret of toppling walls.

God Gives Men Light

An unusual man steps before us. His name frequently appears in the *Caesarea Courier* as one of the city's outstanding citizens. He has an enviable position as commanding officer of one hundred men. The residents of the community know him as a man whose faith has reached his purse, for he is generous. More than that, his prayer life is not neglected, for although he is a Gentile, he has been grasped by the invisible God, to whom his earnest prayers come up as a memorial. What distinguishes this man, Cornelius, from other men of his day? *He has lived up to the light he received from God.*

Paul uses staggering words to deal with this theme: "Because that which may be known of God is manifest in them; for God hath shewed it unto them. For the invisible things of him from the creation of the world are clearly seen, being understood by the things that are made, even his eternal power and Godhead, so that they are without excuse" (Romans 1:19,20).

I have often been asked the question, "What about the heathen who has never had a chance? Is he lost?" According to this great passage of Paul's, there are no heathen who haven't had a chance, for all men are confronted with the light of God in the world of nature, and that light leaves man without excuse.

Cornelius lived up to the light he received, and God cried, "Give that man more light!" This is the genius of outreach. We can say with certainty, based on this portion of the Word, that if men willingly accept the light God has given in creation, then someone will come with more light. Often when traveling on planes and trains I have found a prepared heart, confirming the words, "The preparations of the heart in man, and the answer of the tongue, is from the Lord" (Proverbs 16:1).

After learning the truth that God breaks in upon men with light, we now find that—

God Gives Men Vision

Aren't you impressed as you read God's Word that there is a consistent movement of God in arresting men by vision? Each vision focuses attention upon some special aspect of Deity. Abram saw the faithfulness of God (Genesis 15:1). Elisha saw the sufficiency of God (II Kings 6:13-17). Isaiah saw the holiness of God (Isaiah 6:1-8). Ezekiel saw the sovereignty of God (Ezekiel 1:2-28). Habakkuk saw the program of God (Habakkuk 2:1-14).

In Acts 10 God was about to do the unusual, and in order to accomplish His divine purpose He gave a twofold vision.

To Cornelius. Many guests had dropped in to visit Cornelius, but there had been none like this visitor referred to in Acts 10. Think of it! An angel appeared in his living room to say, "Cornelius, I know you." The God of Heaven dispatched an angel to a Gentile's home to give him *more light.* God could have saved some time if the angel himself had delivered the message to the prepared heart. But no, a man—a human instrument—had to take the message of deliverance to Cornelius.

A great Bible teacher of our day, after fifty years of faithful ministry, made this startling statement: "I have never known anyone to be saved without a human instrument." Scripture confirms this principle in Isaiah 6:8 where the Lord says, "Whom shall

I send, and who will go for us?"

To Peter. It was nearing lunch time and the cook was slow with the "sloppy joes." Peter made his way to the housetop, sat in a lounge chair and fell asleep. When Peter later related this event to those who questioned him, he called what happened to him a *vision* (Acts 11:5). This event indelibly printed upon Peter's mind God's work in this age.

Out of Heaven came a vessel like a great sheet. The vessel touched earth, and as Peter looked he saw "all manner of fourfooted beasts of the earth, and wild beasts, and creeping things, and fowls of the air" (Acts 10:12). When Peter was admonished to "kill and eat," he responded, "Not so, Lord; for I have never eaten anything that is common or unclean." But God had another word for Peter. "What God hath cleansed, that call not thou common."

Three times Peter saw this impressive sheet with its motley congregation, as though God were saying, "Peter, don't forget this!" Peter's mind may have traveled back to the times when the Lord had spoken about "all nations" (Luke 24:47), and about "all that are afar off" (Acts 2:39).

As I stand with Peter on the rooftop and look intently upon all that is taking place, I am impressed with three truths:

The Commencement of the Church

Perhaps this four-cornered sheet with its diversified cargo served as an object lesson to

Peter to show what the church is like and how God brings into it a wide assortment of "creatures" whom He saves by His matchless grace. Let me explain.

The church of Jesus Christ has a heavenly origin. At the very moment Peter saw the descending sheet he may have remembered the day in Caesarea Philippi when he heard the Lord Jesus say, "Upon this rock I will build my church, and the gates of hell shall not prevail against it" (Matthew 16:18).

Paul reminds us of the origin of this unique body, "And to make all men see what is the fellowship of the mystery, which from the beginning of the world hath been hidden in God, who created all things by Jesus Christ" (Ephesians 3:9).

The Continuation of the Church

Peter saw a "great sheet," not a narrow sheet. It was knitted at four corners, for it would reach into the four corners of the world and would take out of the world a people to bear the name of Jesus Christ. For nearly two thousand years the "sheet" has been filling, but yet there is room.

The Consummation of the Church

The church began in the heart of God. Its work is being carried out in history on the earth. A day of completion is coming. The sheet went back to Heaven. Someday the church will be taken up to Heaven to be presented to God Himself, "a glorious church, not having spot, or wrinkle, or any such thing; but that it should be holy and without blemish" (Ephesians 5:27).

The wall of partition that was built strong and high was beginning to crack, because the believers were learning that God gives men light, and He gives men vision. But there is another important phase:

God Gives Men Obedience

One thing is inescapable as you think about what was taking place. The angel appeared to Cornelius and commanded, "Send men to Joppa, and call for one Simon, whose surname is Peter" (Acts 10:5). Cornelius didn't talk back. He obeyed. When Peter arose from his lounge chair, walked back and forth on the rooftop meditating on what he had seen, three men stood at the gate. Cornelius didn't call a committee meeting to help him decide what to do. He just obeyed God. Now what would Peter do? There was a delegation of Gentiles at the door. Would he violate the customs of his people and invite them in? As he stood looking at them he remembered the sheet, and once again there came pressing upon his heart the words, "What God hath cleansed, that call not thou common." Up to this time the welcome mat at Peter's door gave a welcome only to his little clique, his group, but God had done His work, and Peter threw open the door, invited them in, and gave them lodging.

This has to be the focal point of this chapter. Peter has learned that the sheet is "king-sized"—that the Lord is not limited by tradition, prejudice, customs. We, too, need desperately to learn this lesson. God longs to remove the wall and embrace all men. He will accomplish this when we are obedient as Cornelius and Peter were obedient. Dan Crawford once said, "God has a million worlds to do His will, and now and then He finds a man who will obey Him."

We now draw near the house of Cornelius and find that—

God Gives Men a Message

When Peter was summoned by Cornelius, he was expecting to preach a message from God. The three men had emphasized this upon their arrival at Joppa (Acts 10:22). Upon his arrival he found that Cornelius had done his work well, for he found "wall-to-wall people." Cornelius assured him that they had all come with expectation: "Now therefore are we all here present before God, to hear all things that are commanded thee of God" (Acts 10:33).

Isn't it refreshing to hear from Heaven? Peter opened his mouth and delivered the things that God commanded. What great truths are here!

Having taught that *God is no respecter of persons* (verse 34), Peter presented Christ—His death, His resurrection, and His purpose— "that through his name whosoever believeth in him shall receive remission of sins" (verse 43).

The Word of God had done its work. Cornelius and those who were assembled believed, and at that moment "the Holy Ghost fell on all them which heard the word" (verse 44). What had happened? The walls had fallen, the door of faith had been opened to the Gentiles. "Faith cometh by hearing, and hearing by the word of God" (Romans 10:17), and we know that "the Gentiles had also received the word of God" (Acts 11:1). Their reception of the Word and their salvation was followed by obedience to the command to be baptized (Acts 10:48).

The message delivered by Peter is desperately needed by a lost world today. That message is, "Whosoever believeth in him shall receive remission of sins." This is the glad, good news of the gospel that is available and sufficient to all who believe. Let's get past every wall that stands between us and the lost so that we may deliver the gospel to them.

CHAPTER 8
Dynamic Changes

*I*f the early church had published a theological journal, it might well have been called *Changing Times*. Anyone observing the events of Acts' opening chapters must conclude that something was emerging, which was absolutely and utterly unique in history. Changes were taking place—changes that were God-given and God-ordained.

Today change in the church is clamored for. We are urged to *cut loose, streamline, innovate, brighten up* the ministry of the church. However, there does not seem to be a directive from the Head of the church to change the pattern of church life in the twentieth century.

Up to this point in Acts little attention is given to the great company of believers who were affected by the death of Stephen. According to a conservative estimate, there may have been as many as 25,000 believers in Jerusalem at that time. But Saul's outstretched hand against the infant church scattered the seed into distant and safer parts. Luke now reaches back and takes up the historical record: "Now they which were scattered abroad upon the persecution that arose about Stephen travelled as far as Phenice, and Cyprus, and Antioch, preaching the word to none but unto the Jews only" (Acts 11:19).

As they moved out of Jerusalem they went westward to the coastal areas and then followed the highways northward that brought them to Tyre, Sidon, and eventually to the thriving city of Antioch. This was no ordinary city. Its population at that time was over 500,000, and it was rated the third most prominent city in the entire Roman Empire. Only Alexandria and Rome itself outranked her. Beautifully situated on the River Ornotes, Antioch was wealthy and magnificent. It was spoken of as one of the "eyes of Asia." Its main street, four miles long and lined with colonnades, ran straight through the heart of the city.

Cicero describes Antioch as a noble and celebrated place, abounding with learned men and liberal studies. Antioch was a great resort of the Jews because of the toleration that was granted all religions. Rackham, in his *The Acts of the Apostles,* pulls aside the curtains and allows us to look in upon its people: "The one occupation of the Antiochenes was pleasure seeking; and stimulated by the luxurious beauty of the scenery, the mixed population, and the voluptuous character of the oriental worships, such pleasure seeking led to disastrous moral results."

In this city was sown, as the result of persecution, the seed of the gospel. The believers were careful, however, to minister only to the Jews, according to the pattern established at Jerusalem. We remember that on the day of Pentecost Peter directed the message to his own people, saying, "Ye men of Judea" (Acts 2:14), "ye men of Israel" (verse 22), "therefore let all the house of Israel know" (verse 36). This pattern was followed until the ministry to Cornelius.

In this remarkable passage—Acts 11:19-26—Luke shows the changes that were taking place in the life of the church. The norm being established then continues up to this time, and will continue through the rest of the Church Age. We observe first of all the shifts that were taking place, and then we will consider the characteristics of this new movement.

A Shift From Jerusalem to Antioch

In harmony with what Paul later set forth as the divine order for spreading the gospel (Romans 1:16), the early church had preached the gospel first to the Jews. Jerusalem had been "mission headquarters." But revolution was taking place, a mighty change was sweeping through the church, and the center of ministry would soon be Antioch. It was a free city, standing at the crossroads of commerce. Caravans from north, south, east, were funneled into the market places. Sleek sailing vessels waited in her ports to be unloaded and filled again. Transportation would be no problem for the messengers as they thrust forth with the life-changing Word. What a choice place God had selected to be the new center of the church's ministry.

With the change of centers there came also—

A Shift from Apostles to Deacons

This change was inevitable. The qualifications of an apostle could be met only by those who had accompanied the Lord during His ministry and had been eyewitnesses of His resurrection. The one exception to this was Paul, who was appointed an apostle by the Lord after His ascension (Galatians 1:1). The apostolic office was linked with the foundation and establishment of the church (Ephesians 2:20). The qualifications of this office affirm that there are *no* New Testament apostles today.

As the church was prepared for expansion and ministry through the ages, deacons were chosen under divine direction (Acts 6). Lest we might think that this was a specific case or an emergency measure, Paul gave direction to the young man Timothy—and to the church today—about the qualifications of deacons (I Timothy 3:7-13).

In annual meetings our churches do not choose apostles, but we do choose faithful men to be deacons. This is a result of this shift in the early church's life.

We have observed the changes that were God-ordained in the early church. There was a change of place—the church was no longer confined to Jerusalem. Her ministry would go to the "uttermost part." With the change of place came a change in leadership. Now we find that God arranged—

A Change from Jew to Gentile

There has been much discussion, and commentators differ, as to when the men of Cyprus and Cyrene "spake unto the Grecians, preaching the Lord Jesus" (Acts 11:20). It is evident that, up to this time, they had delivered the message to "none but unto the Jews only" (Acts 11:19). Now the Grecians are given the message of the Lord Jesus.

After a rather lengthy discussion of this, Albert Barnes crystalizes the matter by saying, "It is thus manifest that we are here required to understand the Gentiles as those who were addressed by the men of Cyprus and Cyrene" (from *Barnes on the New Testament*).

Having been assured that those who received the message were Gentiles, we are now concerned as to when this event took place. When Luke refers to his writing, he says it was his desire to give an orderly presentation of truth. He introduces his Gospel with these words, "Forasmuch as many have taken in hand to set forth in order...it seemed good to me also, having had perfect understanding of all things from the very first, to write unto thee in order" (Luke 1:1,3). It is reasonable to suppose that the desire carried out in his Gospel is also carried out in Acts, and thus we have a chronological unfolding of the history of the early church. In his *Acts of the Apostles,* G. T. Stokes raises the question: "Was the action of these men of Cyprus and Cyrene quite independent of the action of St. Peter or an immediate result of the same? Our answer to these queries is very short and plain. We think that the preaching of the Hellenists of Cyprus to the Gentiles of Antioch must have been the result of Peter's action at Caesarea, else why did they wait till Antioch was reached to open their mouths to the pagan world?"

The church was advancing. The gates of Hell were being stormed through divinely directed change. Antioch was becoming a center of Gentile evangelization. But other centers would follow because the true headquarters of the church is Heaven (Ephesians 1:21,22; Philippians 3:20).

We have surveyed the changes. We now turn our attention to those practices that marked the church then, and should mark it in this present hour.

The Church at Antioch Was an Evangelistic Church

The word used for *preaching* in Acts 11:20 is related to communicating the good news of Jesus Christ. We see something of the importance of this communication when we find the word used fifty-five times in the New Testament. It was God's intention that gospel preaching would have priority in the church. Frequently we need to remind ourselves that it is not our business to be purveyors of *good advice,* but of *the good news.* Early in my ministry a great evangelist of our country exhorted me, "Don't ever allow your heart to become cold in relation to the preaching of the gospel."

One of the outstanding men of England, D. R. Davies, said, "The Church exists in this world to prepare and save souls for another world. That and nothing else is the business of the church. This, of course, does not mean that the Chruch is not interested in economic and political and social problems, but simply that her interest in economics, politics, sociology, etc., must be conditioned and determined by her primary business of saving souls" (from *Thirty Minutes to Raise the Dead*).

Let us determine to keep our local church alive to the responsibility given her, and let us daily speak to others about Jesus Christ.

The Church at Antioch Was a Faithful Church

When the church at Jerusalem heard that great things were happening at Antioch and that great numbers had turned to the Lord, they did not call a representative from Antioch to Jerusalem for questioning (as they had interrogated Peter about Cornelius), but in their concern sent Barnabas to Antioch. He was "a good man" (Acts 11:24), meaning *a man God-like.* When Barnabas arrived and saw what the grace of God had accomplished, he exhorted them all, "that with purpose of heart they would cleave unto the Lord" (Acts 11:23). The word *cleave* means literally *to abide with.* The indication is that they did just that.

Isn't it a great experience to have a friend who is faithful, someone you can count on regardless of the mess you may be in? God is looking for people He can count on, those He can trust to be faithful in the ordinary tasks.

When Paul wrote to the church at Corinth he reminded them that God required "that a man be found faithful" (I Corinthians 4:2). George H. Morrison once said, "No gifts, no brilliance, no genius can release a man from being faithful. Not in the things we do but how we do them, not in fame but in fidelity, is the true test of every man's work, according to the teaching of our Lord."

As a pastor, I frequently find myself checking the work my church is involved in to see if we are true to the pattern found in this Gentile church. If we are not, then we should take steps to make ourselves an evangelistic church, warm for people, and a faithful church, abiding in the Lord and seeking His will.

The Church at Antioch Made Provision for Growth

With the coming of Barnabas the work grew, and "much people was added unto the

Lord" (Acts 11:24). They were not like those today who say, "Let's keep the church small," or "I like a small church better." God intends that every church should reach its potential, and in order to do this workers are needed.

In the church at Antioch, an immediate church meeting gave Barnabus the signal to "take the bus" to Tarsus and find Paul. Barnabas, who stood with Paul when the Jerusalem church was afraid to have the former persecutor in their pulpit, was the one to find Paul and bring him back to Antioch to be assistant pastor. It is impossible to grow without adequate help, such as Barnabas gave.

Wise is the church that expands to reach the community with the gospel. Don't you long to see the practices of the church at Antioch restored? When we think of *church renewal,* we think of *growth*—the kind the Antioch church expected and allowed for.

The Church at Antioch Was an Instructed Church

Can you imagine a Bible conference lasting a year? Today it's difficult to hold even a three-day meeting. Not so at Antioch. For one whole year Paul and Barnabas taught the Word of God to "much people." The result? "The disciples were called Christians first in Antioch" (Acts 11:26).

W. H. Griffith Thomas states in *Outline Acts,* "The word here translated 'were called,' found only eight times in the New Testament, means in every other place 'voicing of Divine oracle.'" Albert Barnes tells us that "The name was given because they were followers of Christ."

The Church at Antioch Was a Generous Church

The church was scarcely a year old when news came that there was to be a famine "throughout the whole world" (Acts 11:28). The brethren in Judea would be caught in this, they realized, and immediately they received an offering. "Every man according to his ability, determined to send relief unto the brethren which dwelt in Judea" (verse 29). What a blessing it would be if such generosity were present in the churches today!

CHAPTER 9
Divine Intervention

When John Milton sat down to write his immortal *Paradise Lost,* he was caught up in the wonder of God. The opening lines are magnificent:

Of man's first disobedience, and the fruit of that forbidden tree whose mortal taste

Brought death into the world, and all our woe,

With loss of Eden, till one greater man

Restore us, and regain the blissful seat."

As the introduction closes, this blind genius breaks out in prayer, and we hear his supplication to the God for whom he will speak:

What in me is dark illumine,
What is low raise and support;
That, to the heighth of this great
argument,
I may assert Eternal Providence,
And justify the ways of God to men.

We are given the opportunity in Acts 12 to see world rulers, the early church, the individual believer, the powers of Hell, and overshadowing all "the ways of God with men." As the curtain lifts and the scene comes before us, we see

The Providence of God

A frequently asked question is, "Why do things happen as they do? Isn't it unjust for a little baby to be snatched from its mother's arms in death? How can it be right for terminally ill people to live on in pain and suffering?" If there is one truth we need to grasp in our fragmented world today it is the greatness of our God in His providential ways. We need to remember what Augustus Strong wrote in his *Systematic Theology:* "Providence is that continuous agency of God by which He makes all the events of the physical and moral universe fulfil the original design with which He created it."

The church in Acts was experiencing her finest hour. The wall that separated Jew and Gentile had been broken down. "Much people was added unto the Lord" (Acts 11:24), and now Satan moved upon Herod to trouble the church, destroy her leaders, and decimate her power. With violent hands Herod killed James with the sword, and thrust Peter into prison.

How do you explain God's apparent unconcern for James and His care for Peter? They were both men of God. Doesn't God always treat His people the same way? Does He have favorites?

Let's refresh our thinking on this theme of providence. The psalmist observes how God takes care of us in death as well as in life (Psalm 103:3-5,15,16). He understands that this takes place because, "The Lord hath prepared his throne in the heavens; and his kingdom ruleth over all" (Psalm 103:19). The word *all* embraces the totality of things. His providence is evidenced in nature (Genesis 6:17). He brings the rain (Amos 4:7). His providence is displayed over animals. Shem, Ham, Japheth, and their youthful wives didn't chase the animals into the ark; God brought them (Genesis 7:9). And God is provident toward man: "A man's heart deviseth his way: but the Lord directeth his steps" (Proverbs 16:9).

The opening verses of Proverbs 16 tell us that "Man proposes but God disposes." It is evident that man with all his boasted freedom makes plans, but in so doing advances God's designs.

What about our national life? We see God's providential hand in nature, in animals, in man, but it is also good to know that He controls the march of history. This is evidenced in Daniel 4:17. When Nebuchadnezzar wrote his proclamation, he reminded his readers that his position in the nation did not come as a result of his winsome personality or his able campaigning, but from God. "This matter is by the decree of the watchers, and the demand by the word of the holy ones: to the intent that the living may know that the most High ruleth in the kingdom of men, and giveth it to whomsoever he will, and setteth up over it the basest of men." This sounds as though he had been reflecting on the words of Proverbs 21:1: "The king's heart is in the hand of the Lord, as the rivers of water: he turneth it withersoever he will."

When reflecting upon the attempts of Herod to harass the church, remember that he held his position under a God who is sovereign in all His ways. Herod may have been the "basest of men," but things were not out of God's hand. James and Peter, God's servants, were also in that sovereign hand.

Frequently when people come to visit me in hours of apparent tragedy the essence of their cry is, "Explain why James is killed and Peter isn't." I go back to one of the sublime portions of the Bible for an answer. When Abraham was faced with the destruction of a city, his heart was encouraged by his realization: "Shall not the Judge of all the earth do right?" (Genesis 18:25). Regardless of how difficult the circumstances, we can rest with a quiet heart because of God's *rightness*.

James Russel Lowell gave to us a profound word:

Careless seems the great avenger; history's

pages but record

*One death struggle in the darkness 'twixt
old systems and the Word;*

*Truth forever on the scaffold, wrong forever
on the throne,*

*Yet that scaffold sways the future, and
behind the dim unknown*

*Standeth God within the Shadow, keeping
watch above His own."*

—"The Present Crisis" *(Lowell's Poems)*

The Deliberateness of God

Peter was confined in prison (Acts 12:3,4).
He had been in prison before and the prison
doors had popped open and he had been
delivered. The angel of the Lord had slipped
down the airways and opened the doors,
bringing Peter and the others forth and
instructing them, "Go, stand and speak in the
temple to the people all the words of this life"
(Acts 5:20). The authorities who had killed
James with the sword read the news about
Peter's previous excape, and they took
measures to prevent its happening again.
Herod appointed four shifts of four soldiers
each to guard Peter around the clock. But
despite close guarding and a well-secured
prison, there doesn't seem to be the slightest
indication that God had any concern. As the
time before Easter slipped rapidly away,
there was no flashing light, no angel at the
gate. Where was God?

Many Christians collapse at this seemingly
desperate hour. They feel God should have
arrived earlier or that He should have worked

the way they had planned. Sometimes I feel strengthened in my soul when I realize that others, too, have faced delays. Can you imagine Noah's waiting 120 years for judgment on the world? For forty years Moses led the sheep in the back side of the desert (Exodus 3:1). Peter and the other apostles waited most of the night in a storm before anyone came (Matthew 14:22-36). Mary and Martha sent an urgent message to the Lord Jesus saying, "He whom thou lovest is sick" (John 11:3). How frustrated they must have become when He did not arrive until several days later.

As these scenes pass before you, a wonderful truth emerges—*Delays are not denials*. Remember, the flood *did* come. God *did* appear to Moses to deliver him from his loneliness. The Lord Jesus *did* come in that night of storm, and Martha and Mary *did* receive more than they had ever expected. There have been hours when I have needed to reflect again on these strengthening truths. It could be that they can meet your immediate need.

The Ministry of God through Prayer

Have you ever wondered, as you returned home from prayer meeting, if your prayers would really work? Does God really hear and answer prayer? Does prayer actually move the Hand that moves the world? God included this narrative in the heart of Acts that we might never doubt again the efficacy of united prayer. "Peter therefore was kept in prison: but prayer was made without ceasing of the church unto God for him" (Acts 12:5).

When we look in upon this scene we are aware that the church took prayer seriously, for "many were gathered together praying" (verse 12). Don't push this aside. They were asking God to do the impossible, to do what they could never do. They could have gotten out a petition or arranged a march against the government, but they dared to ask God to do what was, for them, impossible.

While the church was at prayer, Heaven was not insensitive. Angels were being briefed to make their rounds. Today many books are being written about angels, but the Bible itself is the best authority on this topic. Sit down sometime with your Bible and concordance and experience the joy of learning about these heavenly citizens who minister to us. The writer of the Hebrew letter asks us, "Are they not all ministering spirits, sent forth to minister for them who shall be heirs of salvation?" (Hebrews 1:14).

The truth of angelic ministry is woven throughout the Word of God. Hagar, pressured by circumstances and running away, was found by an angel (Genesis 16:7). When Israel stood in need of direction, an angel of God was there (Exodus 14:19). When Elijah was despondent and desired to die, an angel brought food to restore him (I Kings 19:5,6). When Shadrach, Meshach and Abednego were tossed into a burning furnace, they discovered that an angel was there ahead of them, and in their desperate hour they were not alone (Daniel 3:28). And would you believe an angel invaded a lions' den and locked the lions' mouths so Daniel would be safe? (Daniel 6:22).

It is interesting to observe that angels do not do for us what we are able to do for ourselves. Peter could not break the chains, so the angel used his strength for that work; but having done that, "the angel said unto him, Gird thyself, and bind on thy sandals. And so he did. And he saith unto him, Cast thy garment about thee, and follow me" (Acts 12:8). We need to be constantly reminded that it is of little value to pray if we are not willing to be used by God to help answer that prayer. If we ask God to touch the hearts of our friends we ought to be aware that we are His finger for that ministry.

All of the events that have taken place so far in Acts lead to this final truth.

God Delivers

As the angel slipped down the corridor of the prison, Peter followed. Iron gates swung open at the angel's touch, and when they reached the last gate it "opened to them of his own accord" (Acts 12:10). As soon as they passed down the street and the angel knew that Peter was in familiar territory, he departed. Standing alone in the cool air Peter came to himself, and looking back confessed: "Now I know of a surety, that the Lord hath sent his angel, and hath delivered me out of the hand of Herod, and from all the expectation of the poeple of the Jews" (verse 11).

The God whom Peter had come to know is not only the God of salvation, but also the God of deliverance. Let's look for a moment at the wonder of this. He delivers us from our hostile environment (Exodus 3:8; 6:6-8). According to Psalm 18:17, He delivers us from our strong enemy. (Aren't you glad the psalmist doesn't specify the enemy? He might have left yours out!) He delivers us from all fears (Psalm 34:4).

Recently I heard a speaker say that man is haunted by at least 200 different fears. I don't know how true this is, but the psalmist says *all* in Psalm 34:4, and that covers it. Notice the same psalm includes *troubles* (verse 17) and *afflictions* (verse 19).

We can apply God's power in delivering Peter to His work of delivering us from sin and from Satan's power. Men are in bondage, and in response to the prayers of God's people are released from the prison of sin. Charles Wesley realized this, and testified,

Long my imprisoned spirit lay
Fast bound in sin and nature's night;
Thine eye diffused a quickening ray,
I woke, the dungeon flamed with light;
My chains fell off, my heart was free;
I rose, went forth, and followed Thee.

CHAPTER 10

Storming Through God's Direction

At the age of 33 Thomas Jefferson assumed the awesome responsibility and honor of presenting to Congress the written document of the Declaration of Independence. The *American Testament* by Irwin Glusker and Richard Ketchum tells how this tall, freckled, sandy-haired man, shy, well-liked by just about everyone, explained his intention. It was: "to place before mankind the common sense of the subject, in terms so plain and firm as to command their assent...it was intended to be an expression of the American mind."

As July 4, 1776 came, and John Hancock signed the document, a nation was born that was destined to become one of the great world powers changing the course of history.

America's strength today can be traced to that eventful hour when God gave direction to those men who were shaping its destiny as an emerging nation.

Great as that hour was, it slips into insignificance in the light of the event before us in Acts 15. The Declaration of Independence dealt with nations and man's relation to man, while the Jerusalem gathering had to do with eternal verities—man's relation to God and the direction God would have the church take as she walked with triumphant tread through the centuries.

Recent events had plummeted the early church into an hour of crisis. Peter, a Jew, had gone to the house of Cornelius and had been scolded later by his associates in Jerusalem. They accused: "Thou wentest in to men uncircumcised, and didst eat with them" (Acts 11:3). The Gentile movement had been spreading. At Antioch, "the hand of the Lord was with them: and a great number believed, and turned unto the Lord" (verse 21). The crisis had deepened, for in Antioch of Pisidia, "almost the whole city [came] together to hear the word of God" (Acts 13:44). The Jews were filled with envy at what was taking place, but Paul and Barnabas reminded them that all that was happening was in God's plan. "It was necessary that the word of God should first have been spoken to you: but seeing ye put it from you, and judge yourselves unworthy of everlasting life, lo, we turn to the Gentiles" (verse 46).

Don't miss the wonder of this passage. It is

a pivotal area in the book of Acts, for at this point Paul and Barnabas unfolded the truth that in going to the Gentiles the Scripture was fully on their side. "For so hath the Lord commanded us, saying, I have set thee to be a light of the Gentiles, that thou shouldest be for salvation unto the ends of the earth" (verse 47).

Israel's rejection had opened the door to wider blessing and glory. When the missionaries finally returned to Antioch, "they rehearsed all that God had done with them, and how he had opened the door of faith unto the Gentiles" (Acts 14:27).

But all that was happening in the spread of the gospel was only deepening the problems. For instance, visitors came down from Jerusalem to Antioch with the charge: "Except ye be circumcised after the manner of Moses, ye cannot be saved" (Acts 15:1). How would Paul and Barnabas handle this problem? They had seen God do a mighty work of salvation among the Gentiles, and now those who seemed to be leaders dared to arise and say that salvation is by ritual.

Luke is careful to inform us that this problem caused more than just a ripple of discord. Note the words he uses in Acts 15:2: "no small dissension and disputation." *Dissension* is translated *insurrection* in Mark 15:7 and *uproar* in Acts 19:40. Paul and Barnabas, therefore, got involved in an extremely volatile debate with the Judaizers from Jerusalem.

Something had to be done to save the

church from fragmenting. So the congregation at Antioch sent representatives— Paul, Barnabas and others—to Jerusalem to help settle once and for all the nagging problems. Three problems needed to be dealt with: doubt about the way of salvation, doubt about the purpose of the church, and doubt about the believer's responsibility.

On their way to Jerusalem, Paul, Barnabas and the other representatives of the church at Antioch passed through Phenice and Samaria. As they did so, they declared the truth that God had broken down the walls that had stood between Jews and Gentiles. They announced that Gentiles were being saved. This announcement produced "great joy unto all the brethren" (Acts 15:3). But they had scarcely been received by the church before the Pharisees were there to again affirm the necessity of rites for salvation and the obligation to keep the Mosaic law.

Have you ever thought how much might be involved in the words that introduce this council in Acts 15:6? Did they have a Scripture reading? Was there an opening prayer; and if so, who led it? Did James announce the restaurants in the area for the noon meal? Who provided the special music? Were the embellishments that we enjoy in our present-day conferences in evidence? While there is much that we do not know, there are great affirmations we *do* know that are as important today as they were then. This was a doubt-removing conference, and great issues were settled.

Removed Doubt Regarding
the Way of Salvation

It is a wholesome exercise to observe Peter in these hours of crisis. On the day of Pentecost we see "Peter, standing up with the eleven" (Acts 2:14). At the house of Cornelius "Peter opened his mouth" (Acts 10:34). (Incidentally, this is a good way to do our preaching and teaching—God save us from mumbling!)

And when the pressure was on and questions were flying about, "Peter rose up, and [spoke] unto them..." (Acts 15:7). Question number one on the agenda was the question of *salvation*. As I look back over the years that God has given me to minister, without any hesitation I can say that this is still the main issue. Are we saved through merit, through rites, through keeping the law? How? We can be glad that Peter rose up that day and made the important announcement that God had chosen him to deliver the message of the gospel to the Gentiles. As he spoke he sent before them words that were crisp, as fresh and vital now in this bewildered age as they were that day at the Jerusalem Conference. Had we been there that day we would have been moved to hear:

The word of "the gospel" (verse 7). We would have said to each other, "God has invaded the world with Good News." This Good News? "That Christ died for our sins according to the scriptures; and that he was buried, and that he rose again the third day according to the scriptures" (I Corinthians 15:3,4). That news is as up to date as today. It doesn't change.

The word "believe" (verse 7). How we need to major once again on this great word. When John wrote his Gospel he stated at the close that out of the many miracles performed by the Lord Jesus he chose specific ones for a purpose: "These are written, that ye might believe that Jesus is the Christ, the Son of God; and that believing ye might have life through his name" (John 20:31).

Upwards of one hundred times the word *believe* is used in John. It is by *believing* that we receive the life-giving water.

The word "purifying" (Acts 15:9). The gospel message, received, brings the results that men long for. A heart purified, a life cleansed, is made possible through the grace that has been manifested in Jesus Christ.

A few years ago a friend involved in government took his two-week vacation and spent it at the Exposition that is held annually in Toronto. He set up his booth on the grounds. Every day he talked with men, and gave out hundreds of pieces of literature. As a result, over two hundred persons lingered to talk with him and to tell him that they were concerned about their salvation but no one had ever made it clear.

There's no reason for us to question how to be saved. This conference in Acts makes it clear. There is *one way* for Jew and Gentile alike. It is the way of faith.

Removed Doubt Regarding
the Work of the Church

If we have any doubt about the relevancy of this, all we need to do is read the deluge of books dealing with this subject. Over and over again in our pastors' conferences this question is foremost. What is the local chruch to do in today's world?

James, the moderator of the Jerusalem meeting, stated with brevity, "Men and brethren, hearken unto me: Simeon hath declared how God at the first did visit the Gentiles. . ." (Acts 15:13,14). James reminded them that their duties included:

The proclamation of a message (verses 15-18). Peter called the message that he delivered "the gospel" (verse 7). Let's look in on another scene where we find the culmination of Peter's word to Cornelius. It is the assurance that because of Christ's death and resurrection, "whosoever believeth in him shall receive remission of sins" (Acts 10:43).

The procuring of a people. Peter had reminded the members of the council that their message would bear results even in Gentiles who bear His name (Acts 15:7,14). The Word indicates that He procures this people for Himself. In this present age God is redeeming a people, which is a work that will go on until "The day of Jesus Christ" (Philippians 1:6). Then will come God's "after this" when Israel will again be on the main line of His purpose.

The primary purpose of the church is the

proclamation of a message, the gospel, which results in the salvaging of a people. The passing centuries have changed neither the nature of man nor his plight. The message that rescued man then is the message that is desperately needed now. So preach it! Teach it! Practice it! Only then will the church gain the attention of the world.

There was yet more work for that first assembly of the church to take care of. They had settled the issue of how men are brought to God; they had removed doubts about the church's purpose. So they turned their attention to the truths that will—

Remove Doubt Regarding
Christian Responsibility

As the conference began, they were faced with the question of "the law of Moses" (Acts 15:5). They could not have the benediction and sing, "God be with you till we meet again," without answering a question that, even today, frequently fragments the church.

What is my Christian responsibility? I have in my library a valuable volume, *The Commandments,* by Maimonides. In this volume Maimonides brings together the commandments given in the Pentateuch. He totals 613: 248 positive and 365 negative. What burdens are laid upon men in this 425-page volume! But the early Jerusalem Conference sought to keep from placing a heavy load upon those who had turned to Christ. In their letter they stated, "It seemed good to the

Holy Ghost, and to us, to lay upon you no greater burden than these necessary things" (Acts 15:28). What was meant—and is meant today—by "these necessary things"? Three great principles are given:

Practice holy living—"Abstain...from fornication" (verse 20). Those who have been reached with the gospel are to abstain from those things that would bring reproach upon the name of the One who bought them. Holy living *is* possible because we are indwelt by a Holy Guest who desires to live the life of Christ through our mortal lives.

Abstain from things strangled, and blood (verse 20). W. H. Griffith Thomas observes that in this, God was teaching the sacredness of human life. What a principle to be heralded today, with death on the highway, violence in the streets, and murder in our homes by men who do not respect the sacredness of life. Our teaching should plead for a restoration of this great principle.

Abstain from idols (verse 20). What an exhortation for this hour. Our culture is geared to the making of idols. Some time ago I asked a friend about another Christian, known at one time to be a man of faith. The answer was brief. "I don't see much of him anymore. He has built for himself some sizable idols. How tragic! We should instead express the desire of the hymn writer:

> *The dearest idol I have known,*
> *Whate'er that idol be,*
> *Help me to tear it from its throne*
> *And worship only Thee.*

CHAPTER 11

Action Through Guidance

During the first evacuation of children from bomb-torn London, a train was ready to pull out of Victoria Station. Many of the children on the train had never ridden one before, and most of them had never been to the country. The parents of a small boy and girl had just said good-bye to their precious children and had left them standing on the platform. The little girl began to cry, saying she was afraid because she did not know where she was going. Her little brother brushed away her tears, put his arm around her to comfort her, and assured, "I do not know where we are going either, but the king knows."

Haven't you had days like that? Circumstances hemmed you in, clouds hung low, and the future seemed so uncertain. Then against the clouds came this rainbow that changed the whole picture. "The King knows."

When Saul met Jesus Christ on the way to Damascus he changed roads. Up to that time he had charted his own course. But now, having been apprehended by God, his future rested squarely in the hands of the One who alone is sovereign.

When we contemplate life with its intricate road system we can be glad that we find encouragement in the vast wealth of Scripture. It comes to us, assuring us that we are not wanderers, but pilgrims traveling on a well-designed course toward a certain destination. Let's gather some of these soul-strengthening promises:

"Thou wilt shew me the path of life: in thy presence is fulness of joy; at thy right hand there are pleasures for evermore" (Psalm 16:11).

"The meek will he guide in judgment: and the meek will he teach his way" (Psalm 25:9).

"Teach me thy way, O Lord, and lead me in a plain path, because of mine enemies" (Pslam 27:11).

"I will instruct thee and teach thee in the way which thou shalt go: I will guide thee with mine eye" (Psalm 32:8).

"Thou shalt guide me with thy counsel, and afterward receive me to glory" (Psalm 73:24).

"For the Lord spake thus to me with a strong hand, and instructed me that I should not walk in the way of this people" (Isaiah 8:11).

These are but a few of a great array of God-given assurances that relate to the difficult area of *guidance*. Most of us know these Scriptures well, don't we? However, even with this knowledge we often find ourselves asking, "How do I make God's promises operative in my daily life?"

It was Thomas Carlyle who observed, "Of all the paths a man could strike into, there is at any given moment a best path for every man—a thing which, here and now, it were of all things wisest for him to do."

Paul's letters often reflect upon the doctrinal and practical aspects of guidance. Note a few of the many references to guidance in his Epistles: Prayer for guidance to Rome (Romans 1:10); God's children are led by His Spirit (Romans 8:14); prayer again for direction to Rome (Romans 15:32); those led by the Spirit are not under law (Galatians 5:18); God was going to undertake the responsibility of bringing Paul to the Thessalonian church (I Thessalonians 3:11).

Having looked at these passages that give us confidence that God does, and will, lead His children, we now give attention to the *how* of guidance. What elements do we find at work in the life of Paul that made God's guidance a practical, day-by-day experience? If we can find the mode of operation for Paul we will have found it for ourselves.

As you have read this delightful book of Acts, you have no doubt found that it is a book of guidance. Philip was guided to leave a great meeting in Samaria and "go toward the south unto the way that goeth down from Jerusalem unto Gaza, which is desert" (Acts 8:26). There was no doubt in Philip's mind that this was God's will, and "he arose and went" (verse 27). Cornelius, an unsaved but concerned man, was guided by God to "send men to Joppa, and call for one Simon, whose surname is Peter" (Acts 10:5). When the men arrived at Peter's apartment, the same Lord who guided Cornelius to send guided Peter to go. "Arise therefore, and get thee down, and go with them, doubting nothing: for I have sent them" (Acts 10:20).

We now focus our attention on a section in Acts where we find great truths to help us in this sticky business of determining the way we should go.

The Word of God

When Paul suggested to Barnabas, "Let us go again," he was moving within the framework of the revealed Word of God. When the church at Antioch met together, a directive was given to them that these two men should go out with the gospel. "And when they had fasted and prayed, and laid their hands on them, they sent them away" (Acts 13:3). Paul and Barnabas were acting in obedience to the word that had been given them.

Our first objective is to discover what the Word of God declares about a given matter. We must not act on our hunches or our feelings, but on that which has been written in the Scriptures. You will recall the words given by the psalmist assuring that God will guide us with His counsel (Psalm 73:24). Literally, he is announcing that God will guide with His Word. There are few areas of our lives that are not dealt with in the Word of God, either by a direct statement or by principles shown in the lives of men and women of faith. It's up to us to find what God has said relative to our intentions.

Let's take a "for instance" just to see how this principle really works. Think of the guidance given by God in relation to our homes, our marriage relations, and our children (Ephesians 5:21—6:4). Here we see God's will, and we should obey it without question.

To enjoy an exciting experience as you study the Word of God, write down the Scriptures that relate to your life, your character and your conduct. Then remember that "If ye know these things, happy are ye if ye do them" (John 13:17).

But let's get back to Paul and Barnabas. Eventually, they had a disagreement. It concerned a young man, John Mark, who was Barnabas' nephew. Paul felt that it was best to leave the young man at Antioch; Barnabas wanted to take him along. It all ended with Barnabas taking John Mark with him in one direction and Paul taking Silas with him as he headed for Syria (Acts 15:36-41).

From Syria, Paul traveled to Derbe, passing through Cilicia. There he added young Timothy to his entourage, and moved on (Acts 16:1-5).

As Paul and his party journeyed over well-marked roads, their plan was to go to Asia

(Acts 16:6). But something happened which frequently occurs in life. There was—

A Barrier

There was no question about Asia's need to hear the Word of God. However, it was not God's plan for them to go to Asia at that time, and in order to direct them He sent interference. "They were forbidden of the Holy Ghost to preach the word in Asia" (Acts 16:6).

When Isaiah spoke about God's guidance in his life, he said, "The Lord spake thus to me with a strong hand, and instructed me" (Isaiah 8:11). David Thomas in his great work on Acts observes, "How the Spirit restrained the apostles from going whither they intended, whether by a revelation, the presence of opposing circumstances, or a mysterious impression which they could not shake off, does not appear. The fact alone is stated—the apostles were prevented by God. They were hindered from carrying out their own volitions. The Divine Spirit is ever restraining men and turning them from their own ways."

Having been prevented from entering Asia, "they assayed to go into Bithynia, but the Spirit suffered them not" (Acts 16:7).

The Outward Circumstance

Paul and his co-workers were not easily turned aside from their plans. The word *assayed* in Acts 16:7 means that *they kept on trying to enter.* But the Holy Spirit would not permit them to go.

We now examine the principle of the closed door. Paul was not a stranger to this, for you will remember that when the apparent blessing of God rested upon his ministry in Damascus, "the Jews took counsel to kill him" (Acts 9:23). When this plan was made known to his friends, they took him by night and let him down over the wall in a basket (verses 24,25). Soon after that he again found this principle at work in his life. He was preaching the gospel with great boldness in Jerusalem when the Grecians planned to kill him. Again the brethren rescued him and bought a ticket for his return to Tarsus (Acts 9:29). A door that had seemed open was abruptly slammed in his face. God was making known to this choice servant an unchanging principle.

Some years ago I became acquainted with a certain man. Although high up in the fields of education and theology, he told me that he always discerned God's guidance by using the principle of the closed door.

God's guidance is always within the framework of His Word. Sometimes there are barriers that obstruct our path. At other times the doors close with no explanation. But we should be aware that the God of the closed door is also the God of—

The Open Door

The experiences Paul and his party went through must have been baffling to them. Why the barriers? Why the circumstances that arose to say, "Don't go this way"? Often

God, in His goodness, allows us to wait, to catch our breath, and to learn the secret of being still. Paul had learned this in earlier days while he was yet Saul. Have you ever thought about the long wait that reaches from Acts 9:30 to Acts 11:25? There is a strange silence about Paul's activities during those years. However, we can be assured that they were not insignificant years.

It could well be that a long period of time will stretch from the time a door slams shut until it opens again on silent hinges. Spurgeon commented on Psalm 37:23: "The steps of a good man are ordered by the Lord." He said, "The stops, too." It may be that at this very moment God is saying to you, "Wait awhile." Remember that even in this God has not forgotten you.

The invisible hand of God had been pushing Paul's party toward the sea. Each time their moves had been thwarted, and now before them loomed a restless, dark expanse of water declaring: "Stop!" That night as they retired their minds were full of questions. What would tomorrow bring? Little did they realize that before the day would break there would be an event of such magnitude that it would change the course of history. That night Paul had a vision. "There stood a man of Macedonia, and prayed him, saying, Come over into Macedonia, and help us" (Acts 16:9).

The cry of a man in the night for help is an experience that can never be pushed aside. The nagging question on their hearts as to the direction they should go was answered by a vision of outstretched hands and a voice crying, "Come!" Here was a representative man who cried for all the men of Macedonia—and for us, for the entry of Europe started Christianity's move westward. Aren't you thankful that without a committee meeting or a pious "We'll pray about it and be in touch with you later," the decision was made? When morning broke they booked passage on the first boat.

In his commentary on Acts, W. Graham Scroggie speaks of this critical hour: "The vision vouchsafed at Troas ushered in the most momentous event in the history of Europe, the going forth of the Gospel to enlighten the nations of the West."

At Troas Dr. Luke joined Paul's group, as indicated by the "we" in Acts 16:10. You can almost hear the group singing as they board ship: "He leadeth me, O blessed thought, O words with Heavenly comfort fraught! What e'er I do, where e'er I be, Still 'tis God's hand that leadeth me." They were confident because of—

Sound Judgment

In Acts 16:10 there is an important word that has much bearing on the direction we take. We cannot help but believe that the four men (Paul, Silas, Timothy and Luke) sat around the table at the restaurant in the very early morning and surveyed once again what had been happening to them. *Assuredly gathering* is a picturesque statement. It means that they laid out on the table everything that had taken place, and one thing came through loud and clear. *All the events pointed in one direction.* They did not act on untested impulses. They weighed the evidence and rejoiced in the guidance that God had given.

It is possible that before this day or week has passed you will be making decisions that will have great bearing on your life. Don't forget these important elements of divine direction—the Word, circumstances, and sound judgment.

CHAPTER 12
Action Through Affirmation

*I*n the year 1795 Timothy Dwight became President of Yale College. As he stepped on to the campus he became aware of impiety, disorder and wickedness. The place was infected with infidelity. Every "up-to-date" student scoffed at the idea of the Bible. It was the glory of Yale men to ridicule the idea of religion. A pitiful minority professed any belief in Christianity, and those who did hardly dared to speak. A small handful attended church. The order of the day was profanity, intemperance and gambling.

Timothy Dwight determined to bring order to Yale and to restore faith in the living God. In an attempt to ridicule him, one of the Literary Societies asked him to speak on the subject, "Are the Scriptures of the Old and New Testaments the Word of God?" The listeners came that day to scoff, but when they left they were amazed at the mighty demonstration of God's power and the clear defense of the Scriptures.

Seven short years later, one third of the student body had come to a personal faith in Christ, and one third of those men had made a choice to enter the ministry. Dwight's soul had been stirred by a need, and the result was an amazing visitation of God.

Hundreds of years before, another man was stirred as he stepped into a culture permeated by idolatry, and he was given the privilege of presenting the living God. The account of his ministry is recorded for us in Acts 17:15-34.

The people who moved up and down the streets of Athens were not aware that on this particular day, a group of believers from Berea had come to the city. They brought with them a man who, in the next few days, would deliver a message that would be read and reread through the passing centuries. The truths of his message would always be relevant. When Paul registered at the motel he reflected on what he had witnessed—men prostrating themselves before idols of their own making. It has been pointed out that there were more idols than men in Athens. It was into this situation that Paul stepped.

He disputed with the citizens in the market place. He encountered Epicureans, who believed that everything happened by chance, that death ended all, and that pleasure was the chief end of man. Along with the Epicureans came the Stoics, who were pantheists and who believed that at death the soul would be burnt or returned to be absorbed in God. A resurrection from the dead, as the gospel declares it, seemed out of the question to the Stoics' thinking.

Can't you imagine the bombshell that was dropped in the midst of their philosophical speculations? A man announced that there was One who had conquered death, was alive, and offered life to all who would believe in Him (John 14:19). As they heard this startling announcement, their interest grew and they wanted to hear more of what the "babbler" would say (Acts 17:18).

This word "babbler," found only here in the New Testament, referred to a small bird that picked up seed for its food. It was also sometimes used of an ill-educated person who picked up bits of wisdom here and there and passed them on with a facade of learning.

"And they took him, and brought him unto Areopagus, saying, May we know what this new doctrine, whereof thou speakest, is? For thou bringest certain strange things to our ears: we would know therefore what these things mean" (Acts 17:19,20).

As Paul was being escorted to the place of his preaching appointment, he walked down the streets where Aristotle, Demosthenes, Plato and Socrates had walked. The hour was ripe for Paul's entrance upon the scene. Thomas Lindsay affirms this in his *The Acts of the Apostles:* "No great thinkers lived, no fresh philosophical thinking remained: the teachers traded in learning, and philosophy had become mere logic-shopping. Men lived in words, careless of real things. The change had not come rapidly. Four centuries earlier

Demosthenes had told his townsmen that they preferred hearing and retailing news to fighting for their liberties. They had become worse in Paul's time, and the whole occupation of Athenians and students who came to finish their education there was to gratify a superficial intellectual curiosity."

The philosophers had walked the streets and taught their students, but men were still bewildered and lost. Paul walked toward Mars' Hill not as a philosopher, but as a man who had met Jesus Christ and had experienced a divine constraint to communicate the message of true life. As Paul stood up to speak in the midst of the crowd on Mars' Hill, he began with courtesy and grace. How else could he speak about the God of grace? I can almost hear him, as a hush falls upon his listeners: "Ye men of Athens, I perceive that in all things ye are too superstitious" (Acts 17:22).

In *Acts—The Expanding Church,* Everett Harrison has observed, "This much debated term could be either a criticism (cf. 'ignorance' in v. 23) in which case 'very superstitious' would be the preferred rendering, or it could be a compliment. The latter is more probable if Paul wished to create a friendly atmosphere for his remarks. But it is not to be construed as flattery, for this was forbidden at hearings conducted by this body, and it was alien to Paul's character."

The altar with the inscription TO THE UNKNOWN GOD (Acts 17:23) had not escaped the searching eyes of the apostle. The altar was saying, with great eloquence, that the gods they knew had never satisfied their deepest longings or needs. Their spiritual capacity had not been filled by the gods of their own making. This was Paul's point of contact. The God they did not know, he knew. He did not say, "I will now define or describe this unknown God," but "him declare I unto you." We are now privileged to reflect upon what, without question, was one of the greatest messages ever delivered. As you read it, take your place with the crowd who were hearing for the first time the wonder of the living God. What does Paul declare about the One he knows?

God Made the World

Imagine how startled the Epicureans would be as they heard Paul's affirmation: "God...made the world and all things therein" (Acts 17:24). They believed creation came by a fortuitous concourse of atoms—the work of chance; while the Stoics held that the universe had existed from eternity. As the men of Athens walked the streets of their city, they saw the clouds in the sky. They felt the patter of rain upon their faces. They observed the starry host of heaven, but they did not recognize that before the design there had been a *Designer*. They did not see that behind all that was made was a *Maker*.

Aren't you amazed when you open your Bible and read, "In the beginning God created" (Genesis 1:1)? Arrested by that statement, you read on through the account of creation. Ten times we see, "And God said." With each statement there is a corresponding result. When God speaks something happens! The psalmist reached back and took hold of these great words in Genesis 1 and said, "By the word of the Lord were the heavens made; and all the host of them by the breath of his mouth....he spake, and it was done; he commanded, and it stood fast" (Psalm 33:6,9).

As Paul, moved by the Spirit of God, began his great treatise to the Romans, he reminded his readers that God had left His stamp upon creation. Every man in the world is guilty in the light of His creative work "because that which may be known of God is manifest in them; for God hath shewed it unto them. For the invisible things of him from the creation of the world are clearly seen, being understood by the things that are made, even his eternal power and Godhead; so that they are without excuse" (Romans 1:19,20). The Athenians and the men of this day alike stand guilty before God because God's revelation of Himself in creation is clearly seen and cries out, "Guilty!"

The God Who Can't Be Measured

The God who created all things cannot be boxed (Acts 17:24b). One of the great dangers in this present hour is that we make God small, anemic, inadequate for our living in a trouble-packed world. Once He presenced Himself in buildings: the tabernacle (Exodus 40:34) and the temple (I Kings 8:11). But now the God of creation, the God who is immeasurable, lives in us. "Know ye not," Paul asked the Corinthian believers in his first letter to them, "that your body is the temple of the Holy Ghost which is in you, which ye have of God, and ye are not your own?" (I Corinthians 6:19). God is not now dwelling in buildings but in bodies—yours and mine.

The tension on Mars' Hill must have been mounting. The God the Athenians did not know, this guest speaker did know and proceeded to show that He is also—

The God Who Directs History

What a faith-inspiring truth! If we do not believe that God is in control of history, as Paul declares in Acts 17:26, and that all history is *His Story,* then we have reason for worrying. Solomon reminds us in Proverbs 21:1, "The king's heart is in the hand of the Lord, as the rivers of water: he turneth it whithersoever he will." Daniel records for us the utterance of King Nebuchadnezzar, "the most High ruleth in the kingdom of men, and giveth it to whomsoever he will" (Daniel 4:25), "and setteth up over it the basest of men" (Daniel 4:17).

He made the nations, according to Paul's testimony in Acts 17:26. The divine hand in this endeavor is manifest in Genesis 10 where we find fifty-eight original nations being placed by God's sovereign hand. A. H. Sayce, in *The Races of the Old Testament,* comments on this chapter: "The ethnologist must be content to leave the sons of Noah to the historian or the theologian. He must start from the fact that they were considered to have settled in each of the three zones of the known world, and that the nations who inhabited these zones at a later day were, according to the idiom of a Semitic language, their children and successors."

He determined their times, according to Acts 17:26. The rise and fall of nations does not come by accident. Their destiny is determined by the God who made them. This truth is the focus of II Chronicles 36:15-21. You can hear the march of the Chaldean army, the roar of planes and tanks, but over it all you read, "Therefore he brought upon them the king of the Chaldees" (verse 17). The armies marched, but God directed them.

He appointed their boundaries. Paul delivered this important fact, too, to the Athenians (Acts 17:26). When Moses was moved to deal with this great truth he said, "When the Most High divided to the nations their inheritance, when he separated the sons of Adam, he set the bounds of the people according to the number of the children of Israel" (Deuteronomy 32:8).

The Mars' Hill crowd was now aware that Paul was dealing with the God of creation and of history, but His dealings soon became very personal. They saw Him as —

The God of Concern

There was movement in this theological message. Everything had been flowing to the fact "That they should seek the Lord, if haply they might feel after him" (Acts 17:27). Paul was asserting what we are all aware of, for within every man there is a God capacity. There is a part of our personalities that is God-shaped, and nothing else can fill the void except God Himself. It cannot be filled with food, with pleasure, with sex, with drink, with dope, with *things*. Men are attempting to fill it in this fragmented world, but all their efforts are vain.

Joseph Parker states that "we ourselves are limited expressions of God—we are made in the image and likeness of the Creator. God has left His witness within ourselves, and if we would fairly and honestly continually study ourselves we would have no difficulty about the Godhead." There is a longing in man's heart for completeness, and that longing comes from the living God, for "in him we live, and move, and have our being" (Acts 17:28). Do you feel as I do about this message? It moves me, it stirs me. I stand in awe as Paul comes to his final words, presenting—

The God Who Will Judge

When Barnabas and Paul ministered at Lystra they made reference to how God "in times past suffered all nations to walk in their own ways" (Acts 14:16). In Romans 3:25 we read of the forbearance of God. And to the philosophers assembled at the Areopagus Paul declared, "The times of this ignorance God winked at; but now commandeth all men everywhere to repent" (Acts 17:30).

Lindsay elaborates, "God does not impute to men errors which they had committed in ignorance; but now that he hath made himself known, ignorance can no longer be pleaded." God has made Himself known, and because of that revelation man is totally responsible. God has stepped forth in history in a Person, and that Person is Jesus Christ. "No man hath seen God at any time; the only begotten Son, which is in the bosom of the Father, he hath declared him" (John 1:18). Yes, God has stepped into history. God has broken into view in Jesus Christ. All judgment has been committed to Him, "For the Father judgeth no man, but hath committed all judgment unto the Son" (John 5:22). The evidence that this has taken place is an empty tomb and a Man, beyond the reach of death, who lives "after the power of an endless life" (Hebrews 7:16).

The Day of Judgment is on God's calendar, and the Judge is already appointed. But the resurrection of Christ carries with it the glad good news of the gospel, for He was "was delivered for our offenses, and was raised again for our justification" (Romans 4:25).

Responses to Paul's invitation were few. Only two names are recorded. Dionysius, a member of the Council, reportedly became a leader in the church at Athens. Damaris, whose life in relation to the church is not known, was the only woman mentioned.

Once again we have learned that *the Word of God does the work of God.* May we learn to trust it as we proclaim it.

Paul moved on from Athens to preach the Word in other places. And as he did so the Roman empire reeled and shook as the gospel of God's saving power made an unforgettable impact. The devil's grasp on men's souls began to slip as the Apostle Paul and other zealous Christians reached out to them and won them to the Saviour who sets the captives free. As the book of Acts closes, we see Paul as a prisoner in Rome, still preaching the gospel. We are not taken beyond this scene by the writer of Acts. And perhaps for good reason. The story of Acts has not ended; the preaching of the gospel is still going on today as redeemed men and women put on the armor of the Lord and *storm the gates of Hell*.

Are you on the Lord's side?